Starry
Speculative
Corpse

[Horror of Philosophy, vol. 2]

Starry Speculative Corpse

[Horror of Philosophy, vol. 2]

Eugene Thacker

Winchester, UK
Washington, USA

First published by Zero Books, 2015
Zero Books is an imprint of John Hunt Publishing Ltd., Laurel House, Station Approach,
Alresford, Hants, SO24 9JH, UK
office1@jhpbooks.net
www.johnhuntpublishing.com
www.zero-books.net

For distributor details and how to order please visit the 'Ordering' section on our website.

Text copyright: Eugene Thacker 2014

ISBN: 978 1 78279 891 0

A CIP catalogue record for this book is available from the British Library.

Design: Stuart Davies

Printed and bound by CPI Group (UK) Ltd, Croydon, CR0 4YY, UK

We operate a distinctive and ethical publishing philosophy in all
areas of our business, from our global network of authors to
production and worldwide distribution.

CONTENTS

Also in the series:

1

Starry Speculative Corpse

Descartes' Demon. Sometime around 1639, René Descartes sat down at his desk to write. At issue for him was a simple question concerning knowledge. Philosophy, theology, mathematics, astronomy, medicine, the arts, and the natural sciences all claim to know things. From them a cumulative understanding of the self, of others, of the world, and of the cosmos is made possible. But how do we know that what we know is actually true? What is the foundation on which these disparate fields of knowledge are based? Are there questions that cannot – or should not – be asked, lest they undermine the knowledge they are designed to produce? How much uncertainty is tolerated before knowledge becomes doubt, and when does doubt come to a stop, if ever?

An abyss opens up. For Descartes this was a personal as well as a philosophical problem. As he writes, "Some years ago I noticed how many false things I had accepted as true in my childhood, and how doubtful were the things that I subsequently built on them and therefore that, once in a lifetime, everything should be completely overturned and I should begin again from the most basic foundations..."[1]

Being the astute thinker that he was, Descartes set out a method for addressing this problem. The task was, as he notes, ambitious, and Descartes writes that he had been waiting for a "mature age" at which to undertake this project. Whether the age of forty-three was the right age or not is hard to say. He felt he had been waiting long enough, even too long, and so, Descartes writes, "today I appropriately cleared my mind of all cares and arranged for myself some time free from interruption. I am alone and, at long last, I will devote myself seriously and freely to this general overturning of my beliefs."[2]

The result of these exercises in skepticism are well known to students of philosophy, and, when *The Meditations on First Philosophy* were published in Paris in 1641, they immediately attracted a whole range of responses, not least of all from the ongoing debates over the relationship between philosophy and theology, reason and faith.

Descartes' most lasting application of his methodological doubt comes in the first of his meditations, where he considers how our senses deceive us. Dreams, hallucinations, painting, and other examples are discussed as instances in which we think we know something based on sensory evidence, and are in fact deceived. But at least in these instances we can learn, from experience, to distinguish dream from reality, and the image from the thing itself. Our senses are reliable, if used properly.

But Descartes pushes his doubt even further. What if our senses are, by definition, deceptive? What if deception is, as it were, hard-wired into our very modes of being? Descartes raises this question through a kind of thought experiment:

> Therefore, I will suppose that, not God who is the source of truth but some evil mind, who is all powerful and cunning, has devoted all their energies to deceiving me. I will imagine that the sky, air, earth, colours, shapes, sounds and everything external to me are nothing more than the creatures of dream by means of which an evil spirit entraps my credulity. I shall imagine myself as if I had no hands, no eyes, no flesh, no blood, no senses at all, but as if my beliefs in all these things were false.[3]

Another abyss opens. Often dubbed the "evil demon" or "evil genius," here we see Descartes pushing his doubt to an extreme point, a point at which no knowledge is possible because nothing is for certain. One thought is as good or as bad as another, everything relative, arbitrary, haphazard, pointless. Subject to continual deception, prey to the cunning of unknown entities, dismembered and insubstantial, Descartes has let himself to stand on the precipice of philosophy and peer over the edge. And what he finds there is a terrifying abyss, where there is neither certitude nor knowledge, nor even a single thought – just a tenebrous, impassive silence.

"But this is a tiring project and a kind of laziness brings me back to what is more habitual in my life." Can we blame Descartes for stepping back from the precipice? Thinking is hard work, yes, but the negation of all thought is, perhaps, harder. What Descartes inadvertently discovers is at once the ground and the greatest threat to philosophy, the question that cannot be asked without undermining the idea of philosophy itself.

Traditionally, the Socratic tradition in philosophy has a thera-peutic function, which is to dispel the horrors of the unknown through reasoned argument. What cannot be tolerated in this tradition is the possibility of a world that cannot be known, or a world that is indifferent to our elaborate knowledge-producing schemes. Descartes' *Meditations* begin – and end – in this mode. But along the way there are gaps, fissures, and lacunae in the philosophical edifice. With the evil demon Descartes stumbles upon a horror intrinsic to philosophy: the thought that philosophy cannot think without undermining and annulling itself. In order to continue its work, philosophy must ignore it, or gloss it over, or skip it altogether.

And so, in the following meditation, a foundation is provided by Descartes, in his famous formulation *cogito ergo sum*: "...let him deceive me as much as he wishes, he will never bring it about that I am nothing as long as I think I am something. Thus, having weighed up everything adequately, it must finally be state that this proposition 'I am, I exist' is necessarily true whenever it is stated by me or conceived in my mind."[4] From this flows an entire legacy of philosophical thinking, in terms of Cartesian space, Cartesian dualism, and the privileging of human consciousness over all other forms of being.

But it is not so easy to shake Descartes' demon, which continues to haunt his philosophical treatise to the end. It is always there, threatening to undermine whatever conceptual edifice Descartes has constructed. Better to not deal with it at all – and continue philosophizing. Descartes even confesses: "I am like a prisoner who happens to enjoy an imaginary freedom in his dreams and who subsequently begins to suspect that he is asleep and, afraid of being awakened, conspires silently with his agreeable illusions."[5]

* * *

Kant's Depression. On the 12th of February, 1804, Immanuel Kant lay on his deathbed. "His eye was rigid, and his face and lips became discoloured by a cadaverous pallor."[6] A few days following his death, his head was shaved, and "a plaster cast was taken, not a mask merely, but a cast of the whole head, designed to enrich the craniological collection of Dr. Gall," a local physician. The corpse of Kant was made up and dressed appropriately, and, according to some accounts, throngs of visitors came day and night. "Everybody was anxious to avail himself of the last opportunity he would have for entitling himself to say, 'I too have seen Kant.'"[7] Their impressions seemed to be at once reverent and grotesque. "Great was the astonishment of all people at the meagreness of Kant's appearance; and it was universally agreed that a corpse so wasted and fleshless had never been beheld."[8] Accompanied by the church bells of Königsberg, Kant's corpse was carried from his home by torchlight, to a candle-lit cathedral, whose Gothic arches and spires were perhaps reminiscent of the philosopher's elaborate, vaulted books.

In his book *A Short History of Decay*, E.M. Cioran once wrote: "I turned away from philosophy when it became impossible to discover in Kant any human weakness, any authentic accent of melancholy, in Kant and in all the philosophers."[9] Indeed, for many, the name of Immanuel Kant has become synonymous with a certain type of elaborate, grand, system-building philosophy that characterizes works such as *The Critique of Pure Reason*, first published in 1781. Indeed, so decisive was the impact of Kant's later, "critical" philosophy that textbooks on the history of philosophy often refer to philosophy before Kant and "post-Kantian philosophy." The significance of Kant's philosophy is, however, counter-balanced by its notorious difficulty. Reading through the table of contents alone, with its dazzling and labyrinthine array of sections, sub-sections, and sub-sub-sections, is a task in and of itself. Nevertheless, if Kant's philosophy achieved one thing, it was a renewed optimism in philosophy, much in line with Enlightenment ideals concerning the advantages of secular reason and the "maturing" of humanity as a whole. Reading through Kant's works, with their patient and rigorous divisions and sub-divisions, there is a sense of philosophy as an all-encompassing, totalizing endeavor. Philosophy, in its Kantian modes, knows everything – it even knows what it doesn't know.

That Kant suffered from depression may come as a surprise, especially given the ambition of his philosophical books and the enthusiasm of his wide-ranging intellectual interests (his lecture courses cover everything from philosophical logic to anthropology to chemistry to predictions about the end of the world). But in 1798, in a letter to a colleague on the topic of "the art of prolonging human life," Kant commented on his own struggle with depression. The comments are rare for Kant, both in the sense of being personal and in the way they serve as a confession of weakness. In typical fashion, Kant first defines depression as "the weakness of abandoning oneself despondently to general morbid feelings that have no definite object (and so making no attempt to master them by reason)."[10] A thought without an object is a troubling thing in Kant's philosophy; it can lead to endless train of fickle thoughts without any ground, similar to the speculative debates in Kant's time over the existence of God, the origin of the universe, or the existence of a soul. Reason becomes employed for no reason – or at least, for no good reason. At issue for Kant is not just the employment of reason over faith or imagination, but the instrumental use of reason – reason mastering itself, including its own limitations. This was as much the case for everyday thought as it was for philosophical thinking: "The opposite of the mind's self-mastery... is faint-hearted brooding about the ills that could befall one, and that one would not be able to withstand if they should come."[11]

And when the coherence of reason is threatened, so is philosophy. Or rather, so is the philosopher. A little later on, Kant offers this strange confession: "I myself have a natural disposition to hypochrondria because of my flat and narrow chest, which leaves little room for the movement of the heart and lungs; and in my earlier years this disposition made me almost weary of life."[12]

Elsewhere Kant drops hints of this depression. In the *Critique of Judgement*, for instance, he allows that "misanthropy" is preferable, and even has the character of the sublime: "Falsehood, ingratitude, injustice, the puerility of the ends which we ourselves look upon as great and momentous... these all so contradict the idea of what men might be if they only would, and are so at variance with our active wish to see them better, that, to avoid hating where one cannot love, it seems but a slight sacrifice to forego all the joys of fellowship with our kind."[13]

But Kant does not give in so easily to this "pathology" of thought. Philosophy is the panacea. Kant distinguishes "philoso-phizing" from "philosophy," though both play a therapeutic role in reason's self-mastery. Philosophizing, for Kant, "does not involve being a philosopher," but instead "is a means of warding off many disagreeable feelings and, besides, a stimulant to the mind that introduces an interest into its occupations."[14] At another level, there is "philosophy" proper, "whose interest is the entire final end of reason (an absolute unity)," and which "brings with it a feeling of power which can well compensate to some degree for the physical weaknesses of old age by a rational estimation of life's value."[15]

This is all fine, from the critical distance of philosophical self-mastery. But things get a little more complicated when Kant discusses depression (in the same essay he also discusses boredom, diet, and sleep). What Kant doesn't consider is that reason might actually be connected to depression, rather than stand as its opposite. What if depression – reason's failure to achieve self-mastery – is not the failure of reason but instead the result of reason? What if human reason works "too well," and brings us to conclusions that are anathema to the existence of human beings? What we would have is a "cold rationalism," shoring up the anthropocentric conceits of the philosophical endeavor, showing us an anonymous, faceless world impervious to our hopes and desires. And, in spite of Kant's life-long dedication to philosophy and the Enlightenment project, in several of his writings he allows himself to give voice to this cold rationalism. In his essay on Leibniz's optimism he questions the rationale of an all-knowing God that is at once beneficent towards humanity but also allows human beings to destroy each other.[16] And in his essay "The End of All Things" Kant not only questions humanity's dominion over the world, but he also questions our presumption to know that – and if – the world will end at all: "But why do human beings expect an end to the world at all? And if this is conceded to them, why must it be a terrible end?"[17]

The implication in these and other comments by Kant is that reason and the "rational estimation of life's value" may not have our own best interests in mind, and the self-mastery of reason may not coincide with the self-mastery of us as human beings (or, indeed, of the species as a whole). Philosophical reason taken to these lengths would not only make philosophy improbable (for how could one have philosophy without philosophers?), but also impractical (and what would be the use of such a "depressive reason"?). What Kant refers to as depression is simply this stark realization: that thought is only incidentally human. It would take a later generation of philosophers to derive the conclusion of this: that thought thinks us, not the reverse.

Legend has it that Kant's final word on his deathbed was "enough" (*genug*).[18] The aged peripatetic philosopher of Köningsberg let out a word that was also a sigh, and depressive reason seems to have had the final say.[19]

* * *

Nietzsche's Laughter. Nothing is more indicative of human culture than the obsessiveness with which it has depicted its own planet. When the Earth was decentered from the universe by Copernican astronomy, this was more than compensated for by the innumerable images of the Earth produced over the years by artists and scientists alike. The Earth was, and is, in many ways, still at the center of things. In this sense, the first televised images of the Earth can no doubt be regarded as the pinnacle of a species solipsism, one that has its underside in the many computerized film images of a disaster-worn, zombie-ridden, apocalyptic landscape. We are so fixated on the Earth – that is, on ourselves – that we would rather have a ruined Earth than no Earth at all.

Astronauts often refer to their first view of Earth as the "overview effect," suggesting that the view of the Earth from space produces a shift in consciousness – that we as human beings are not separate from the planet on which we live. The general message is that of sublime wonder and unity: national boundaries disappear, and over its surface the planet reveals strange, luminous patterns of color, cloud, and light (otherwise known as cities, smog, and the electrical grid). Thanks to digital technology the overview effect can now be an everyday experience.

However, in its appeal for a planetary consciousness, the overview effect tends to reveal something different – the indifference of the planet vis-à-vis our repeated attempts to render it meaningful. It is in this context that one is reminded of Nietzsche's oft-quoted passage from "On Truth and Lie in an Extra-Moral Sense":

> In some remote corner of the universe, poured out and glittering in innumerable solar systems, there once was a star on which clever animals invented knowledge. That was the haughtiest and most mendacious minute of "world history" – yet only a minute. After nature had drawn a few breaths the star grew cold, and the clever animals had to die.[20]

Here Nietzsche gives us a different take on the "overview effect." In this version, we have never been one with the planet, nor does the planet require our cleverness and technical ingenuity to save it – from ourselves. It is tempting to imagine Nietzsche himself as a present-day astronaut, going up into space, turning back and seeing the Earth, and noticing the contrast between the indifferent, glittering planet and the equal indifference of the busy and clever animals on its surface. No doubt Nietzsche's ill-health would mean that he would fail to complete the astronaut training. And so he would settle for writing it down.

But Nietzsche's capacity for undermining the human is perhaps needed now more than ever. On the one hand, we who are still on the Earth's surface cannot escape an awareness of the impact of climate change, beset as we are by disasters that increasingly refuse the distinction between the natural and human-made. On the other hand, the process of recuperating the planet for us as human beings continues unabated. Whether we can "save" the planet is one question – whether the planet needs saving is another.

Nietzsche encapsulated this dilemma in the title of his third published book: *Human, All Too Human*, a book that captures the polyphony of voices in Nietzsche's writing – by turns sarcastic, enthusiastic, naive, spiteful, meditative, joyful.[21] For example, in the second volume of *Human, All Too Human*, Nietzsche gives us yet another, much more sardonic variant on the overview effect:

> There would have to be creatures of more spirit than human beings, simply in order to savor the humor that lies in humans seeing themselves as the purpose of the whole existing world and in humanity being seriously satisfied only with the prospect of a world-mission. If a god did create the world, he created humans as *god's apes*, as a continual cause for amusement in his all-too-lengthy eternity... Our uniqueness in the world! alas, it is too improbable a thing! The astronomers, who sometimes really are granted a field of vision detached from the earth, intimate that the drop of *life* in the world is without significance for the total character of the immense ocean of becoming and passing away... The ant in the forest perhaps imagines just as strongly that it is the goal and purpose for the existence of the forest when we in our imagination tie the downfall of humanity almost involuntarily to the downfall of the earth...[22]

As Nietzsche jibes, the strange endeavor of human thinking tends to eclipse the world, until we become so philosophically solipsistic that even the non-human – by its very name – begins to look a lot like the human. Nietzsche caps off his rant with the following: "Even the most dispassionate astronomer can himself scarcely feel the earth without life in any other way than as the gleaming and floating gravesite of humanity."[23]

But Nietzsche's phrase *Menschliches, Allzumenschliches* has several meanings. Certainly it evokes a sense of disappointment – the "all too human" as less than human, as the failure to live up to the various standards, criteria, and values that we associate with being human. And, as Nietzsche repeatedly points out in his book, this itself has become a hallmark of the human. But the phrase also evokes a more critical sense of failing to challenge our most basic and habitual ways of thinking and living – including the questioning of those same criteria and values that demarcate the human from the non-human.

At the same time, Nietzsche's invectives against humanity are outstripped only by his refusal to dispense with the term "human," much less imagine a romantic, transcendent realm "beyond" the human – itself the height of humanist thinking. Nietzsche repeatedly affirms this notion of the human, all too human, even as he rails against it. Human beings are all too human not only because we fail to live up to the human – and what we assume it means to be human – but because we are merely human, only human, and in a way that refuses both the divine *fiat* of science as well as the natural history of religion's chosen peoples. This is Nietzsche's own, tragi-comic brand of humanism: *that there is nothing special about the human.*

When Nietzsche began writing *Human, All Too Human* around 1876, many changes were afoot – the thirty-two year old philologist was forced to retire from his teaching post at the University of Basel due to a series of health issues, which included stomach problems, arthritis, migraines, nausea, vomiting, and rapidly deteriorating eyesight. He had also alienated himself from Wagner and his cultist circle, opting instead for the life of an itinerant scholar. Deciding to relocate to a better climate, he traveled to Sorrento, where he wrote the bulk of the first volume of *Human, All Too Human.* 1878 saw the publication of *Human, All Too Human: A Book for Free Spirits,* comprising some 600 aphorisms. Of the 1000 copies printed, only 120 sold – the remaining volumes were subsequently rebound together with the second volume for the 1886 edition.[24] The following year another four hundred aphorisms would be published with the title *Assorted Opinions and Maxims,* and the year after that, another 350 aphorisms with the title *The Wanderer and His Shadow.* Writing in *Ecce Homo* some twelve years after its initial publication, Nietzsche would characterize the book as "the monument of a crisis" and a "spiritual cure."

The change in lifestyle was echoed in Nietzsche's writing style as well. While in Sorrento, Nietzsche began writing in the brief, aphoristic style that would characterize some of his best-known works. But Nietzsche's aphorisms are not of a single mold, and his turn to the short form manifests itself in different ways, from mini-essays in the vein of Montaigne to taut maxims reminiscent of La Rochefoucauld. We also get dialogues, parables, poetry, even jokes. Indeed, *Human, All Too Human* not only reflects Nietzsche's experiment with style, but with reading as well. One anecdote has Nietzsche reading La Rochefoucauld's *Sentences et maximes* on the train to Sorrento, but Nietzsche himself gives the detective in us a number of clues: in addition to scholarly works on Greek tragedy and philology, Nietzsche is reading Chamfort, Lichtenberg, Montaigne, Pascal, Vauvenargues, Voltaire (the dedicatee of the first edition of *Human, All Too Human*), and of course Schopenhauer, ever Nietzsche's "educator" and paragon of misanthropic aphorisms.

Human, All Too Human is a master class in fragmentary writing, an exegesis on the virtues of the "incomplete thought," as prescient today in our era of the "overview effect" as it was in Nietzsche's era of Darwinism, the Industrial Revolution, and Spiritualism. It is no accident that such experiments in the incomplete thought take as their subject the problem of the human. Above all, the phrase "human, all too human" signals the beginning of a trajectory that would reach across all of Nietzsche's writings, and would continue into the rediscovery of his work by generations of twentieth-century philosophers and theorists. The "overview effect" rendered as the "gleaming and floating gravesite of humanity."

Were Nietzsche writing today, he might very well regard the flora and fauna of contemporary philosophy (posthuman, transhuman, inhuman, non-human, and so on) as so many varieties of this impulse to redeem the human, through the back door, the side door, a trap door... But Nietzsche himself was not immune to such impulses. For every misanthropic statement there is a statement of almost ecstatic, almost embarrassing affirmation, and for every impulse to start a project there is the equal impulse to abandon it. An entry from Nietzsche's notebook in the fall of 1878 simply reads: "A novel. A volume of poetry. A history. A philology." An entry from the summer of 1879, perhaps during a bout of illness, reads: "All I lack is a homunculus." Another note, from the fall of 1879, reads: "I am thinking of having a long sleep." In his notebook, Nietzsche puts the phrase itself in quotes, but does not give a reference.

* * *

Horror of Philosophy. When Descartes stumbles across his demon, he discovers a thought that potentially undermines his entire philosophical project. A dilemma presents itself. If Descartes accepts the demon as actual, he has remained true to his method of skeptical doubt – but then his project is futile, since there is no ground for his thoughts, and nothing can be known for certain. If Descartes rejects the demon, either by ignoring it or by glossing it over, he can carry on with his philosophy, but he has effectively abandoned the original impetus behind his philosophizing to begin with. And so philosophy becomes a kind of pantomime, the passing of time, wasted energy. Either way, it seems that philosophy has to confront the real possibility of its futility – and the equal possibility that one will never know for sure whether philosophy has been futile or not.

This is the crux of the "horror of philosophy," which we see in Descartes' demon, Kant's depression, and Nietzsche's wrestling with an indifferent cosmos. Put simply, it is the thought that undermines itself, in thought. Thought that stumbles over itself, at the edge of an abyss. That moment when the philosopher stumbles upon (Descartes), or cannot avoid (Kant), or actively confronts (Nietzsche) the very thing that undermines their activity as philosophers. Being philosophers, they cannot simply switch tracks, and opt for poetry or mathematics. So they continue the labor of philosophy, all the while under the tenebrous, impersonal gaze of the horror of philosophy.

Far from dismissing philosophy, I would argue that this makes philosophy interesting. Particularly if one "mis-reads" philosophy in this way. If we were to adopt a method, it might be this: read works of philosophy as if they were works of horror. Of course, this is not to ignore the differences between, say, the narrative fiction of Poe or Lovecraft and the analytic, discursive language of Plato or Kant. But, at the same time, we know that many philosophers make use of literary elements (Plato's dialogues being a prime example, not to mention Augustine's use of autobiography and Kierkegaard's use of the parable). And we know that many of the classics of the horror genre, from Poe to Lovecraft to the "new weird" in fiction, are largely idea-driven stories and make extensive use of the discursive mode in their narration or dialogue. One imagines Descartes, the accidental necromancer, making hesitant pacts with demons; one imagines Kant, swaying before the looming abyss of a gothic maelstrom; one imagines Nietzsche, reveling in the *fin-de-siècle* extinction of the species and the attendant exhaustion of vampiric thought.

The proposition that governs this book, *Starry Speculative Corpse*, is that something interesting happens when one takes philosophy not as a heroic feat of explaining everything, but as the confrontation with this thought that undermines thought, this philosophy of futility. Certainly, there is a bit of tongue-in-cheek in this method of reading philosophy as if it were horror; and, like all methods, it is not to be taken too seriously. But the focus in the sections that follow will be on those moments when philosophy reveals the thought that undermines it as philosophy, when the philosopher confronts this thought that cannot be thought.

Admittedly, the title of this series of books – *Horror of Philosophy* – is a bit odd; in one sense, it is something of a joke. Anyone who has, as a student, been forced to read a philosopher like Kant (or worse, Hegel), has no doubt felt a certain horror of philosophy. The sheer heft of a book like *The Critique of Pure Reason* is intimidating in and of itself, never mind the pages upon pages of jargon-filled divisions and sub-divisions that make a mockery of any notion of "plain language" or "common sense." Much of philosophy today prides itself on instilling this intellectual horror in the reader – it is too serious to be taken lightly, too full of gravitas to joke about, replete with relevance, rigor, authority. But this is not just limited to the obscure corners of academic philosophy; our public intellectuals and pop philosophers also leverage this intimidation factor in the guise of the know-it-all, the self-help guru, the philosopher as the person authorized to say something about everything, obliging us to stroke our collective beards in rehearsed gestures of profundity. As a reader, my reaction is something out of a B-horror movie – I recoil in terror.

But if the phrase "horror of philosophy" is a joke, it is because it simply reverses the phrase "philosophy of horror," thereby pointing to a basic assumption we have about philosophy itself.[25] A "philosophy of horror" implies a relation between philosophy and its object. Specifically, that philosophy will either explain its object (whereas in itself it is confusing), give meaning to its object (whereas in itself it lacks meaning), or render its object clear, apparent, and transparent (whereas in itself it is opaque

15

and hidden). This applies to any formula of the type "philosophy of X" where X is philosophy's object, an object that stands apart from philosophy, and because of this, can be analyzed, unpacked, and dissected. Today we not only have the philosophy of religion, the philosophy of nature, the philosophy of mathematics, and political, ethical, and moral philosophy, but also the philosophy of cognition, the philosophy of technology – even the philosophy of... philosophy (that is, meta-philosophy).

Questions arise. Is philosophy's object always separate from it? What happens when the critical distance of philosophy collapses? Does philosophy really have the ability to explain everything? Is philosophy's specialization its universality? And if philosophy can't explain everything, how would we know this, and what language would be appropriate for expressing it? At what point does a philosophy of futility become indistinguishable from the futility of philosophy?

The three volumes of the series aim to take up these questions in different ways, using different forms borrowed from the history of philosophy. The first volume – *In the Dust of This Planet* – introduces the general themes, particularly regarding the limits of the human and the idea of the "world-without-us." This volume – *Starry Speculative Corpse* – aims to, as I've said, read philosophy as if it were horror, while the third volume – *Tentacles Longer Than Night* – aims to do the reverse, to read works of the horror genre as if they were works of philosophy.

2

Prayers for Darkness

Afraid of the Dark. Nearly everyone can relate, I suspect, to the feeling of being "afraid of the dark." Sometimes we may be scared of some unnameable thing *in* the dark, while at other times we may simply be scared *of* the dark itself. As children, we sense this even in the comfort and security of our own rooms, where a dark hallway or open closet may necessitate a whole apparatus of night lights and other talismans, in order to ward off what H.P. Lovecraft once called the "whisperer in the darkness." It is no doubt for this reason that darkness saturates the horror genre, from the earliest examples of gothic novels and graveyard poetry, to the most recent films, comics, and video games. We do not know what it is that dwells in the darkness, only that our not-knowing is a source of fear. In short, our fear of the dark seems as ambiguous as darkness itself.

Indeed, in our everyday usage of the term, "darkness" carries with it a string of associated but different connotations: There is an empirical connotation, in which darkness simply describes the optics or the physics of light. There is the moral or theological connotation of good vs. evil, light vs. dark forces (as when one crosses over to the perennial dark side). Closely tied to this is the epistemological connotation of knowledge vs. ignorance, the enlightened subject vs. the dark savage, that Copernican shift from out of the Dark Ages into an entire epoch of mature Enlightenment.

However, all of these connotations point back to a philosophical dyad, and that is the distinction between presence and absence, being and non-being. Darkness is at once something negative, and yet, presenting itself as such, is also something positive; from a philosophical perspective, darkness exists, but its existence is always tenuous, the stuff of shadows, night, and tenebrous clouds. Darkness "is" but also "is not" – and, in a way, this "is not" also "is" darkness. Put simply, the concept of darkness invites us to think about this basic philosophical dilemma of a nothing that is a something.

Our aim in this chapter is simple: to trace this dual aspect of darkness, the darkness that "is" and that "is not." To do so, we will stray from the straight and narrow path of philosophy proper, into the adjacent territory of mysticism both premodern and postmodern. Here I need to ask patience of the reader. For many of us, the term "mysticism" is too over-coded in our culture, evoking religious cults, New Age fads, astrology readings, drug-fueled hallucinations, and existential tourism in India. The term is, to be sure, too broad to have any specific definition. In addition, even if one limits the term to a particular historical and religious tradition – say, Sufi mystical poetry or the Soto Zen tradition in Buddhism – what one finds is a Pandora's box of different sects, schools, and traditions of practice. The more one searches for "mysticism" in the concrete, the more abstract and amorphous it becomes.

In the first volume of this series, *In the Dust of This Planet*, I attempted to introduce a comparative approach, juxtaposing, for instance, the philosophy of Kant and Schopenhauer to modern Buddhist thinkers such as Keiji Nishitani. But this sort of gesture just touches the surface of the complexities involved in a comparative approach. Here we will try another approach, which is to identify one tradition that has defined itself both as "mystical" and also as a tradition – that of medieval Christian mysticism. The title of one treatise – *The Mystical Theology* – probably written in the late fifth or early sixth century, establishes a tradition that thinks of the divine in terms of motifs of darkness, shadow, abyss, and clouds. Subsequent theologians and mystics refer back to this text – and to each other – in effect contributing to this genealogy of darkness, up to the present day. Importantly, while these thinkers never question their faith, their texts and their ideas also exist in an uneasy relationship to "official," orthodox Christianity. In some cases – as with Meister Eckhart – their ideas invite accusations of heresy, while in other cases – as with Bataille – their so-called mysticism is founded on a radical notion of atheism.

To state the obvious, one need not be "mystical" or religious to appreciate the ways in which these texts take up the philosophical problematic of darkness (that is "is" and "is not"). Of course, these texts need to be understood in the context of Christianity, particularly medieval Christianity, but they need not be totally determined by them. Our own reading – or rather, our mis-reading – of these mystical texts will be a bit "irreligious." We will focus on those moments when darkness comes to define a notion of the divine that is highly ambivalent, contradictory, and radically non-human – and remarkably resonant with the ambivalent, contradictory, and non-human aspects of darkness in the horror genre. As it turns out, to be afraid of the dark may have a mystical impulse at its core.

* * *

Tomb of Heaven. Our starting point – and we will be working backwards from here – is the work of French thinker Georges Bataille. From the time when Bataille, as a teenager, entered a Catholic seminary (which he subsequently abandoned), to his later experiments with the secret society Ácephale, to his last writings on religious art, one can trace the themes of mysticism, darkness, and negation running through nearly all of Bataille's writings. This is especially the case during the 1940s, when, in the depths of the bombed ruins of Paris, Bataille began work on what was to be his magnum opus, which he titled *La somme athéologique*, or the *Atheological Summa*. Given Bataille's dislike of systems, the project was doomed to remain incomplete. The parts that Bataille did publish include the books *Inner Experience* (1943/54), *Guilty* (1944), and *On Nietzsche* (1945). These are eclectic, heterogeneous writings; in addition to philosophical argument, they contain poetry, journal entries, autobiography, and fictional narrative. Jean-Luc Nancy calls them "anti-generic" texts, in that they resist categorization. But I would suggest that, in their form and content, these texts borrow heavily from a mystical tradition that, in the West, extends back to the 5th century, and for which the motif of "darkness" is central.

But Bataille does not simply return to the old forms of mystical thought, either to revive religious faith, or to praise the wonder of scientific modernity. In Bataille's hands, the concept of darkness denotes not just ignorance or the lack of knowledge, but the blind spot of knowledge, the blind spot that in fact inhabits *all* knowledge, the absolute limit that creeps beneath the surface of every relative limit.

There are numerous moments when Bataille resorts to the language of darkness to describe what appear to be extreme experiential states, states akin to the spiritual crises of mysticism:

> But how even for a moment can I dismiss this unknowing (*ignorance*), a feeling of having lost my way in some underground tunnel? To me this world, the planet, the starry sky, are just a grave (I don't know if I'm suffocating here, if I'm crying or becoming some kind of incomprehensible sun). Even war can't light up a darkness (*une nuit*) that is this total.[26]

In passages like this, even experience seems to fail to give testimony to the limit that Bataille experiences – even the heavens are, for him, a tomb, enclosing everything in the enigmatic abyss of incomprehensibility, of impossibility. It is not so much that language fails to adequately describe experience, but that experience fails to adequately circumscribe the human. The boundaries of the human seems to become fuzzy and obscure, at once tomb-like and yet planetary and even cosmic.

What I would like to do is to trace this motif of darkness in a few mystical texts. These texts arguably form a tradition within mystical discourse, a tradition we might simply call "darkness-mysticism." My choices here are, of course, highly selective, and I in no way mean this as a comprehensive survey. Each example puts forth a concept of *negation* that is tied in some way to the motif of *darkness*... though darkness is not always negative for each of these thinkers. And, extending Bataille's ideas, one of the guiding questions for me here is whether it is possible to have, today, a mysticism without God, a negative mysticism, or, really, a mysticism of the unhuman...

* * *

Divine Darkness (Dionysius the Areopagite). Our next stop is an author about whom almost nothing is known – Dionysius the Areopagite, whose short and influential treatise *The Mystical Theology* was produced sometime in the early 6th century. This text, only five pages long, has cast a shadow over mystical writing in the West; it was translated into Latin in the early 9th century, and by the 13th century was a textbook of theology at the University of Paris. Nearly every mystical thinker makes some reference to Dionysius, though the only thing we are sure of is that he is not the person he claims to be.

From the very first lines of the text Dionysius introduces a concept of darkness that is defined by its duplicity. He will often use phrases such as "brilliant darkness" to describe the encounter with the divine:

By an undivided and absolute abandonment of yourself and everything, shedding all and freed from all, you will be uplifted to the ray of the divine darkness which is above everything that is.[27]

In a complex and enigmatic phrase, the author repeatedly asks how we can know the "ray of divine darkness" (Θειου σκοτους ακτινα). Dionysius presumes a concept of darkness that is neither simply privative nor oppositional. In addition, this move – describing the divine in terms of darkness – already sets Dionysius apart from other mystical thinkers of his time, where the encounter with the divine is often described in the more familiar terms of light, illumination, or radiation.

Coupled with this duplicitous concept of darkness is a concept of negation. In the *Mystical Theology* Dionysius outlines two paths of mystical knowledge: an affirmative path, or the *via affirmativa*, and a negative path, or the *via negativa*. In the former one arrives at knowledge of the divine through successive affirmations, as when one describes individual human acts as "good" but the divine as "the Good" or "Goodness" in itself. The latter approach is the opposite, arriving at the divine through successive negations, as when one describes the divine as that which is not created or not existing in time. For Dionysius it is this second path, the *via negativa*, that yields the most profound results, and this is based on the author's fundamental metaphysical commitment to a concept of the divine that is absolutely inaccessible. As he notes, "[s]ince the Divine is the Cause of all beings, we should posit and ascribe to it all the affirmations we make in regard to beings, and, more appropriately, we should negate all these affirmations, since it surpasses all being."[28]

So Dionysius gives us a concept of darkness that is characterized by a duplicity (being at once absence and presence), and along with that, a concept of negation that involves the "negation of affirmations." When we put these two together, what we get is a dialectics of darkness that, in *The Mystical Theology*, moves through stages. An example of this comes from a passage where Dionysius is discussing Moses' ascent of Mount Sinai, a passage that has become something of a touchstone for mystical texts.

There Dionysius begins by describing Moses' initial mystical experience as "seeing many lights, pure and with rays streaming abundantly." Then, at the summit of the mountain, a different type of experience occurs:

...then he [Moses] breaks free of them, away from what sees and is seen, and he plunges into the truly mysterious darkness of unknowing. Here, renouncing all that the mind may conceive, wrapped entirely in the intangible and the invisible, he belongs completely to that which is beyond everything. Here, being neither oneself nor someone else, one is supremely united to the completely unknown by an inactivity of all knowledge, and knows beyond the mind by knowing nothing.[29]

Through a successive stripping away of attributes, through the negation of affirmation, Dionysius puts forth a concept of darkness that is, first, an anti-empirical one (in that one moves away from what is seen and sensed), and then an anti-idealist one (in that one moves away from what can be conceptualized and thought), before arriving at a stage the author can only describe as "unknowing."

With Dionysius, we see a dialectics of darkness that moves from a concept of darkness as privative, to a concept of darkness as oppositional, and finally to a concept of darkness as superlative, and it is in the last type of darkness – a darkness that Dionysius claims is beyond privation or opposition – that we see darkness as a superlative or "divine darkness." This brings one up against a certain limit, not just of language, but of thought as well:

The fact is that the more we take flight upward, the more our words are confined to the ideas we are capable of forming; so that now as we plunge into that darkness which is beyond intellect, we shall find ourselves not simply running short of words but actually speechless and unknowing.[30]

As Vladimir Lossky puts it in his classic study of Dionysius, "the apophatic way, or mystical theology... has for its object God, in so far as He is absolutely incomprehensible."[31]

Now, in spite of the fact that Dionysius brings us to the point of silence, where there is nothing to say, this has obviously not had the effect of silencing mystical discourse. In fact, the opposite is the case. A thinker like Meister Eckhart will take Dionysius' notion that there is nothing to say quite literally – as in, "nothing" or "nothingness" is the only thing that there is to speak of, when one speaks of the divine.

* * *

The Dark God (Meister Eckhart). Working in both the vernacular German as well as the scholastic Latin, writing both popular sermons as well as academic treatises, tried for heresy and claimed by many modern scholars as a Western Buddhist, Eckhart's output is emblematic of the flourishing of mystical thought in late 13th and early 14th century Germany.

Eckhart's notion of darkness is as compounded as that of Dionysius. In his sermons, Eckhart often discusses the difference between God and the Godhead. If God is the divine as it appears to us as human beings, then the Godhead would be that part of God that does not appear to us, and that, therefore, we can never know or experience. Here Eckhart uses the motifs of light and darkness in a fairly conventional manner, as in this passage: "If God is to shine directly in you, your natural light cannot help toward this end. Instead, it must become pure nothing and go out of itself altogether, and *then* God can shine in with His light..."[32]

We should note here that Eckhart's God is the God of the philosophers – non-anthropomorphic, abstract, and metaphysical. If the knowledge of the divine is light, then the knowledge of the senses can only obscure and throw one into darkness. But this sensory darkness gives way to another, more mystical darkness, whereby the self is emptied and negated. For Eckhart, it is only by becoming nothing that one is able to receive the knowledge of divine light. As he notes, "you cannot do better than to place yourself in darkness and in unknowing." Paradoxically, one must become absolutely dark, in order to become light:

> So in truth, no creaturely skill, nor your own wisdom, nor all your knowledge can enable you to know God divinely. For you to know God in God's way, your knowing must become a pure unknowing, and a forgetting of yourself and all creatures.[33]

But the problem is that the divine, in Eckhart's formulation, cannot really be parceled out in this manner, for the divine is a flowing and unbroken continuity, not a Janus-faced God. Thus God is not one part seen, and one part unseen; instead God is the manifestation of the divine to us that radiates or emanates from the Godhead as its source. In this more Neoplatonic interpretation, God emerges from the Godhead. The problem here, of course, is that this implies that God is in fact created from the Godhead, which not only goes against the very definition of the divine, but also puts one in the Aristotelian dilemma of "turtles all the way down."

Be that as it may, it is important to Eckhart to highlight these two dimensions to the divine – one side as outpouring manifestation, and one side as a kind of primordial darkness or unmanifestation. Eckhart attempts to grapple with this problem with the following cryptic statement:

> The final end of being is the darkness or nescience of the

hidden Godhead whose light illumines it, but this darkness comprehends it not.[34]

This passage is complicated, even frustrating. It is also emblematic of Eckhart's polyvalent usage of the term "darkness." In the first part of the sentence, darkness appears to describe the Godhead, which is "dark" because it is "hidden" or inaccessible to us as human beings. All that remains of this inaccessible Godhead is its hiddenness, and thus we gain a residual access to this inaccessibility, a residual knowledge of our inability to know: "darkness or nescience…"

But is this darkness equal to mystical knowledge? That is, does the darkness lead one to what Dionysius calls "unknowing"? On the one hand it does, because, this darkness is described by Eckhart as the final end and goal of all being – thus the culmination of all being is darkness, or this enigmatic knowledge of that which can never be known.

On the other hand, in the second part of the sentence, Eckhart adds that this hidden, "dark" Godhead is also radiating light that illuminates the human subject – that same subject that can only know the impossibility of knowing. There seems to be a disconnect here, a sort of mystical miscommunication, as the Godhead radiates light, but the human only receives darkness. Here "darkness" is not the mystical unknowing described by Dionysius, but the failure of knowledge, mystical or otherwise – "the darkness comprehends it not."

It seems, then, that Eckhart's notion of darkness is a highly conciliatory one. Unable to fully comprehend the divine light in itself, we as humans are stuck with this inability – indeed, we are abandoned to this inability, a dark knowing that follows in the Dionysian tradition of unknowing – the human knowing the absolute limit of all human knowing.

* * *

In and With Darkness (Angela of Foligno). The next stop in our itinerary is Angela of Foligno, a 13th century mystic whose major work, *The Memorial,* was written as dictation by a Franciscan monk known as "Brother Arnaldo," who became Angela's confessor. Angela is, along with Mechthild of Madgeburg, Hadewijch, and Marguerite Porete, one of the central female figures in the history of Christian mysticism.[35] For the better part of her life, she lives what amounts to a respectable, middle-class existence; born in the Italian town of Foligno, just outside of Assisi, she marries young, bears several children, and manages a household. Around her thirty-seventh year, however, she enters a period of intense spiritual crisis. It leads her to seek the spiritual counsel of a local Franciscan monk and to undergo a lengthy period of penance. Intelligent, passionate, and independent, she vows to transform her life, renouncing her material possessions, her social status, and her family life. Eventually she gives away all her belongings, literally stripping herself bare before the crucified body of Christ. She undertakes a diligent practice of prayer, alternately weeping and mortifying her own flesh. On a pilgrimage to Assisi with Brother Arnaldo in the fall of 1291, she experiences several visions, which so fill her with the divine that, when the visions depart, she shrieks and collapses – in her own words, her joints become dislocated, the flesh torn from her body, and she screams continually for death to take her. Arnaldo, somewhat dismayed by the episode, is at first embarrassed, and then confused. Is Angela possessed by an evil spirit, or has she really received divine visions? Arnaldo proposes that Angela tell him everything that has happened, and over the next few years, from 1292 to 1296, the still-perplexed monk writes down Angela's own words, as well as his own commentary. The resultant text – *The Memorial* – outlines a mystical itinerary that includes nineteen stages, with seven supplementary stages, beginning with Angela's conversion and concluding with a fascinating discussion on the experience of the divine in terms of its darkness.[36]

Angela's version of divine darkness, though it bears resemblance to Dionysius and Eckhart, is also remarkably different. Her visions are more intense, more sensationalistic even, but they also convey an ecstatic joy that is often coupled with images of mortality, corporeal decay, and death. Her visions emphasize the material aspect of mysticism in images that appear to the modern reader as starkly morbid and gothic. In one vision, Angela, while in prayer, is invited by Christ on the cross to drink the blood from his wounds: "...I saw and drank the blood, which was freshly flowing from his side... And at this I began to experience a great joy..."[37] Another vision, again while in prayer, has Angela literally going into the open wound in the torso of the crucified Christ: "...it seems to my soul that it enters Christ's side, and this is a source of great joy and delight."[38] In yet another vision, Angela finds herself in the tomb with Christ, in a kind of necrophilic embrace: "She [Angela] said she had first of all kissed Christ's breast – and saw that he lay dead, with his eyes closed – then she kissed his mouth, from which, she added, a delightful fragrance emanated... Her joy was immense and indescribable."[39]

Grotesque as they seem, such images participate in a broader iconography of Christ's body during the Passion, and modern scholars have detected allusions in *The Memorial* to everything from Dante to the *Song of Songs*. It is this material mysticism that works its way into Angela's comments on the divine darkness. There are, of course, passages in which Angela talks about "darkness" in a privative sense, and associates it with human finitude, desire, and temptation. For instance, in the Sixth Supplementary Step, Angela describes all the various doubts and challenges to her faith as "this most horrible darkness":

When I am in this most horrible darkness caused by demons it seems to me that there is nothing I can hope for... When I am in that darkness I think I would prefer to be burned that to suffer such afflictions. I even cry out for death to come in whatever form God would grant it.[40]

Importantly, the darkness that Angela here describes is not limited to those moments of temptation, vice, or wrong-doing. That is, it is not just a moral darkness, in which darkness is aligned with "evil" acts and impure thoughts. Angela implies that it is also part and parcel of being a mortal creature, of existing in a body that is "in such pain and so weary of life that it is ready to give itself up." It is a metaphysical darkness, the suffering of the body's cadaverous facticity, of a body so easily and effortlessly reduced to mere matter. This is a darkness only resolved by death.

This leads Angela – in the Seventh and final Supplementary Step – to comment on another type of darkness. This time darkness is not privative, not the absence or the taking-away of something. More in line with the Dionysian tradition, darkness is here equivalent to a non-anthropomorphic notion of the divine. Angela relates the shift in perspective after this turning point:

Afterwards I saw him in a darkness, and in a darkness precisely because the good that he is, is far too great to be conceived or understood... And in this most efficacious good seen in this darkness now resides my most firm hope, one in which I am totally recollected and secure.[41]

Angela's tone is markedly different – more confident, more self-assured, more steadfast in her faith. And yet what she is expressing is something enigmatic, something that she herself places at the limits of language and thought. This is not the darkness of the decaying cadaver, of something reduced to nothing, but rather the darkness of the divine, of something that is "nothing" because it so far surpasses anything.

Importantly, Angela qualifies this by noting that the divine is "dark" not only because it surpasses human comprehension, but because in so doing it renders the human insignificant. In the divine darkness one enters the divine abyss of oblivion, in which the human being annihilates itself in an ambiguous and yet ecstatic joy: "When I am in that darkness I do not remember anything about anything human, or the God-man, or anything which has a form. Nevertheless, I see all and I see nothing."[42]

* * *

Dark Contemplation (The Cloud of Unknowing). Though little is known about the author of the 14th century Middle English text *The Cloud of Unknowing*, it remains one of the most significant expressions of the darkness-mysticism tradition in the English language. According to scholars, *The Cloud* was written as a spiritual guidebook, though whether for monks or laypersons is unclear. But its focus on asceticism and contemplation is unmistakable, as is its influence of mystical theologians such as Dionysius the Areopagite. *The Cloud* itself cites Dionysius' *The Mystical Theology*, and contains numerous parallels to Dionysian commentators such as John Scottus Eriugena, Thomas Gallus, and the theologians at the Abbot of St. Victor.

The Cloud is first and foremost a practical text. Throughout its chapters it emphasizes the idea of asceticism in its root meaning, as spiritual exercise, covering everything from the reading of scripture, to techniques for prayer, to bodily discipline and warning novices against "unseemly outward behavior." But it is also a highly expressive text, evoking abstract, difficult images of opacity, shadows, and of course darkness. *The Cloud* is an example of what scholars have referred to as "affective Dionysianism," a mixture of poetic and theological ruminations on the divine as inaccessible, incomprehensible, radically non-human. At its most intense, *The Cloud* advocates for a spiritual exercise that entails a successive stripping away of the self, so that it may be ready to encounter the impersonal, formless "cloud" of the divine.

At the center of *The Cloud* is a distinction between two types of "clouds," the "cloud of forgetting" and the "cloud of unknowing." Both are prerequisites for the spiritual life, and both involve mediations – one between the self and the world, and the other between the self and God:

> If ever you come to this cloud, and live and work in it as I bid you, just as this cloud of unknowing is above you, between you and your God, in the same way you must put beneath you a cloud of forgetting, between you and all the creatures that have ever been made.[43]

Here we have two forms of negation, resulting in two types of darkness. For the spiritual novice, one negates one's relationship to the world through refusal and renunciation, thereby establishing a cloud of forgetting. One may be *in* the world but one is not *of* the world. This in turn leads the novice to the divine, but here confronted as a limit: "For when you first begin to undertake it [the spiritual exercise], all that you find is a darkness, a sort of cloud of unknowing; you cannot tell what it is, except that you experience in your will a simple reaching out to God."[44] Having renounced the world, the novice is left in a kind of limbo, cast adrift without direction. And, importantly, there is no simple resolution, wherein one finds again a new ground; the limbo is perpetual. It is this limbo, this darkness, that *The Cloud* points to as the divine:

> Now when I call this exercise a darkness or a cloud, do not think that it is a cloud formed out of the vapours which float in the air, or a darkness such as you have in your house at night... When I say "darkness," I mean a privation of

knowing, just as whatever you do not know or have forgotten is dark to you, because you do not see it with your spiritual eyes...[45]

Taking up some of the themes found in Dionysius the Areopagite, *The Cloud* combines two types of darkness into one: the darkness of human knowledge ("darkness" as privative, as a limit between the known and unknown) and the darkness of God ("darkness" as superlative, as beyond what can possibly be known by human beings).

Much of this is readily in line with Dionysius and his commentators. But where *The Cloud* takes a novel turn is in linking this notion of darkness – as both the limit of thought, and as indicator of that which is forever outside of thought – with contemplation. The Latin term *contemplatio* has a rich history in medieval mysticism, and *The Cloud* references it frequently. But if *The Cloud* never states that the divine can be fully known, neither does it simply opt for an ineffable, transcendent silence. Instead, in a striking passage, it names "contemplation" that enigmatic thought that is also the limit of thought:

> But now you put to me a question and say, "How might I think of him in himself, and what is he?" And to this I can only answer thus: "I have no idea." For with your question you have brought me into that same darkness, into that same cloud of unknowing where I would you were yourself... Therefore, it is my wish to leave everything that I can think of and choose for my love the thing that I cannot think.[46]

I love what I cannot think. Perhaps there is no better formulation for the philosophical impulse in these religious, mystical texts. Thought questions, develops, and is led to a point where thought can no longer continue without negating itself. I love what I cannot think. Perhaps this is also an accurate formulation of the "horror of philosophy."

* * *

The Dark Night (John of the Cross). This preoccupation with the limit of the human finds one of its most dramatic manifestations in John of the Cross, the 16th century Spanish Carmelite monk and mystic, whose collaboration with Theresa of Avila and subsequent imprisonment has become the stuff of hagiographic myth.

John is mostly known for his poem *The Dark Night of the Soul*, as well as its accompanying commentary. Like Dionysius, John thinks of the divine in terms of darkness and negation, resulting in a mystical unknowing of the divine in its inaccessibility. Like Eckhart, John focuses on the processes of darkening and emptying of the human subject as it attempts to comprehend the divine. But John also places a premium on experience – and in particular on the *limits* of experience. Much of this comes from John's more streamlined typology, which distinguishes between two types of darkness:

> This night, which as we say is contemplation, causes two kinds of darkness or purgation in spiritual persons... Hence one night of purgation will be sensory, by which the senses are purged and accommodated to the spirit; and the other night or purgation will be spiritual, by which the spirit is purged and denuded as well as accommodated and prepared for union with God through love.[47]

Here John condenses Eckhart's typology into a kind of pre-Cartesian dualism of flesh and spirit, at once metaphysical and erotic. Both flesh and spirit must be negated in order to comprehend a third type of darkness that John never directly names or discusses. Again, as with Eckhart, the sensory and spiritual annihilation hints at an anti-empirical and anti-idealist thread in the concept of darkness. The darkness of the senses is a pretext to the darkness of the soul, but even this is negated – in John's language, it is "purged" or "emptied" – which then leads to the limit that both Dionysius and Eckhart describe as divine darkness.

Dereliction, abandonment, and abjection are the order of the day in John's writings. As he notes, "the dark night with its aridities and voids is the means to the knowledge of God and self..."[48] But here we risk a great misunderstanding if we read John as advocating a direct, human experience of the divine. For John, mystical experience does not reaffirm or bolster the human subject; quite the opposite. Mystical experience is precisely that which cannot be experienced – the *impossibility* of experience. This point is made more clearly when John hints at a third type of darkness that lies beyond the darkness of the senses or the soul:

> the clearer and more obvious divine things are in themselves, the darker and more hidden they are to the soul naturally... Hence when the divine light of contemplation strikes souls not yet entirely illumined, it causes spiritual darkness, for it not only surpasses them but also deprives and darkens their act of understanding. This is why St. Dionysius and other mystical theologians call this infused contemplation a ray of darkness...[49]

Utilizing Dionysius' phrase "divine darkness," John describes a process whereby both senses and soul are muted, submerged, and finally emptied altogether. Instead of the experience of darkness, what John describes is more like the darkness of experience.

* * *

34

Excess of Darkness (Georges Bataille). John's evocation of the dark night and the impossibility of its experience brings us back to the work of Bataille. As I've mentioned, Bataille's lifelong engagement with the themes of mysticism manifested itself in a range of ways, from his writing, to collective ritual, to his practice of yoga and meditation. We also know that Bataille worked for the better part of his career as a librarian at the Bibliothèque Nationale in Paris, where he specialized in medieval manuscripts and numismatics. Bataille also made use of the library for his own research. Thanks to the bibliomania of Bataille's editors, the final volume of Bataille's complete works contains a catalog of nearly every book he requested from the library. There we see that, during the time in which he was working on the *Atheological Summa*, Bataille is reading Dionysius, Eckhart, Angela di Foligno, John of the Cross, and Theresa of Avila, among many others. These influences can be readily detected in the pages of Bataille's book *Inner Experience*:

> I read in Denys l'Aréopagite: "Those who by an inward cessation of all intellectual functioning enter into an intimate union with ineffable light... only speak of God by negation"... So is it from the moment that it is experience and not presupposition which reveals (to such an extent that, in the eyes of the latter, light is "a ray of darkness"; he would go so far as to say, in the tradition of Eckhart: "God is Nothingness"). But positive theology – founded on the revelation of the scriptures – is not in accord with this negative experience... In the same way, I hold the apprehension of God... to be an obstacle in the movement which carries us to the more obscure apprehension of *unknowing* (*l'inconnu*): of a presence which is no longer in any way distinct from an absence.[50]

Bataille's mystical writings are not simply a ventriloquizing of earlier mystical authors, and neither are they about the existentialist crisis of the modern subject; for Bataille this type of darkness runs the gamut from the most basic forms of "base materialism" and inorganic matter, to the planetary and even cosmic cycles of production, accumulation, and expenditure. That is, this darkness-mysticism has to be placed in the context of Bataille's own version of political economy, a non-human, "general economy" based on excess and expenditure. *In the same way that divine darkness is in excess of the individuated human being, so is there a divine darkness that is in excess of the world – at least the world that we as human beings construct for ourselves and fashion in our image.* Divine darkness is precisely this negative movement that cuts across self and world, the human and the non-human – not by virtue of a bountiful, vitalistic life-force, but by way of an emptying and a darkening. In an almost Lovecraftian vein, Bataille notes that, "beyond our immediate ends, humanity's activity in fact pursues the useless and infinite fulfillment of the universe."[51]

It is interesting to note that Bataille often chooses to express this type of planetary and cosmic darkness in his poetry. But for Bataille poetry is far from being the romantic expression of a brooding subjectivity – he even titles one of his books *Haine de la poèsie*. Instead, poetry for Bataille is related to its ancient roots as *poiesis*, as an anonymous, impersonal producing or creating. The following, for instance, is from Bataille's poem "*L'Archangélique*":

I am the dead man
the blind man
the shadow without air

like rivers in the sea
sound and light
lose themselves in me without end

I am the father
and the tomb
of the sky

the excess of darkness
is the flash of a star
the cold of the tomb is a die

death rolls the die
and the bottom of the heavens rejoice
the night that falls inside me[52]

Far from the baroque, purple prose of the Surrealists, Bataille's poetry displays the sort of minimalism one also finds in John of the Cross. Bataille's concept of darkness maximizes the contradictions already found in Dionysius. The "I" of the poem immediately dissolves into a kind of planetary, climatological material, just as the anonymous, base materialism of the world courses through and is inseparable from the "I". But this is no hippie love-in. For Bataille, as for Dionysius, Eckhart, and John of the Cross, all roads of the *via negativa* lead to darkness, an absolute limit to the human capacity to know itself and the world, a limit Bataille nicely encapsulates in the phrase, "the excess of darkness."

This is where Bataille parts ways with the other mystical thinkers I've mentioned. After Nietzsche's proclamation of the death of God, it would seem that there can no longer be any mysticism. Though profoundly influenced by Nietzsche, Bataille disputes this, opting instead for a mysticism without God, or a mysticism that negates God – but also a mysticism without the human. Bataille's mysticism is no revived humanism – far from it. What remains in Bataille's darkness-mysticism is neither human nor divine, but simply darkness itself. The shift from the earlier mystics to Bataille is akin to the shift from the horror of something in the dark, to the horror of darkness itself. As Bataille notes, in one of his last works: "What I suddenly saw, and what imprisoned me in anguish – but which at the same time delivered me from it – was the identity of these perfect contraries, divine ecstasy and its opposite, extreme horror."[53]

If, for Bataille, darkness is related to mysticism, then it would have to be a darkness that, paradoxically, cannot be thought as such. This type of darkness is not simply privation or opposition, but a darkness that lies at the horizon of the human itself:

I imagine that it is as in vision, which is rendered sharp in darkness by the dilation of a pupil. Here darkness (*l'obscurité*) is not the absence of light (or of sound) but absorption into the outside (*dehors*).[54]

Now, this "outside" that Bataille evokes is not some utopic other place, much less the experience of a transcendent beyond – that is, this darkness that is "outside" is not "above" or "beyond." It is a limit that is co-extensive with the human, at its limit. And this is why I think Bataille's unfinished project is interesting. It does not attempt to pass beyond the human, whether we call it the posthuman or the transhuman. It also does not attempt to undermine the human, be it in terms of objects, actants, or technics. It is perhaps nearer to Nietzsche's call to "pass over" the human, though even this is too optimistic, too messianic, for Bataille. I would suggest that, in borrowing from the darkness-mystical tradition, Bataille's texts opt to darken the human, to un-do the human by paradoxically revealing the shadows and nothingness at its core, to move not towards a renewed knowledge of the human, but towards something we can only call an unknowing of the human, or really, the *unhuman*. Bataille's mysticism, then, is a mysticism of the limits of the human, and this divine darkness would be something like a mysticism of the unhuman.

* * *

An Exegesis on Divine Darkness. Here we can pause a bit and attempt a summary of the ground we've covered thus far. In thinking about darkness (that which "is" and "is not"), we see mystical thinkers connecting a logic (in particular, a logic of negation) with a poetics (a poetics of darkness, shadow, abyss, and the like). With Dionysius the Areopagite the logic of the *via negativa* is tied to his notion of divine darkness (Θειον σκοτους ακτινα). With Meister Eckhart, a logic of negating negations (*negatio negationis*) is tied to the darkness (*finsternis*) of the Godhead, something echoed in the corporeal negations of Angela of Foligno, and the emphasis in *The Cloud of Unknowing* on a paradoxical contemplation of which cannot be thought. In John of the Cross, a negation of all possible experience (including that of darkness) is tied to this central poetic motif of the dark night (*la noche oscura*). And finally, in Bataille, a complex logic of excess and leads to what he terms the excess of darkness (*l'excès des ténèbres*).

What should we make of this tradition of darkness-mysticism. Even though each of these thinkers uses slightly different terms, I would suggest that there are three basic modes of darkness in this mystical tradition: a dialectical darkness, a superlative darkness, and what I've been calling a divine darkness.

The first mode – dialectical darkness – entails a concept of darkness that is inseparable from an opposing term, whatever that term may be. Dialectical darkness is therefore structured around the dyad of dark/light, which finds its avatars in the epistemological dyad of knowledge/ignorance, the metaphysical dyad of presence/absence, and the theological dyad of gift/privation. Dialectical darkness always subsumes darkness within its opposing term, and in this sense, darkness is always subordinate to something that opposes or comes after darkness. With dialectical darkness, the movement is from a negative to an affirmative experience of the divine, from the absence of any experience at all to a fully present experience. However, at the same time, this affirmative experience comes at the cost of a surreptitious negation: a "vision" (*visio*) that is also blindness, an ecstasy (*ecstasis*) or standing outside oneself that displaces the subject, and a rapture (*raptus*) in which the self is snatched away into a liminal otherness. We should note that the recuperative power of dialectical darkness is such that it inhabits all attempts to think a concept of darkness – even those that claim to pass beyond oppositions. Dialectical darkness is at once the ground of, and the obstacle for, any concept of darkness.

This management of boundaries shifts a bit when we move to superlative darkness, the second mode. Superlative darkness is a darkness precisely because it lies beyond the dialectical opposition of dark and light. Paradoxically, superlative darkness surpasses all attempts to directly or affirmatively know the divine. Hence superlative darkness contains a philosophical commitment to superlative transcendence. Superlative darkness makes an anti-empiricist claim, in that it is beyond any experience of light or dark. It also makes an anti-idealist claim, in that it is beyond any conception of light or dark. What results are contradictory, superlative concepts of "light beyond light," the "brilliant darkness," or the "ray of divine darkness." With superlative darkness, there is a movement from an affirmative to a superlative experience of the divine, from a simple affirmation to an affirmation beyond all affirmation. Claiming to move beyond both experience and thought, superlative darkness harbors within itself an anti-humanism (beyond creaturely experience, beyond human thought), leading to a "superlative darkness" or, really, a kataphatic darkness. We should note that with superlative darkness we are brought to a certain limit, not only of language but of thought itself. The motif of darkness comes in here to indicate this limit. And it is a horizon that haunts every concept of darkness, the possibility of thinking the impossible.

This play between the possible and impossible finally brings us to the third mode – what we've been calling divine darkness. Divine darkness questions the metaphysical commitment of superlative darkness, and really this means questioning its fidelity to the principle of sufficient reason. Now, the interesting thing about superlative darkness is that, while it may subscribe to a minimal version of the principle of sufficient reason, it does not presume that we as human beings can have a knowledge of this reason. That everything that exists has a reason for existing may be the case, but whether or not we can know this reason is another matter altogether. Superlative darkness is thus an attenuated variant of the principle of sufficient reason.

Perhaps we should really call this the *principle of sufficient divinity*. The principle of sufficient divinity is composed of two statements: a statement on being, which states that something exists, even though that something may not be known by us (and is therefore "nothing" for us as human beings), and a statement on logic, which states that that something-that-exists is ordered and thus intelligible (though perhaps not intelligible to us as human beings). Superlative darkness still relies on a limit of the human as a guarantee of the transcendent being and logic of the divine, or that which is outside-the-human. The limit of human knowing becomes a kind of back-door means of knowing human limits, resulting in the sort of conciliatory knowledge one finds in many mystical texts.

Now, a divine darkness would take this and make of it a limit as well. This involves distinguishing two types of limit within darkness-mysticism generally speaking. There is, firstly, the limit of human knowing. Darkness is the limit of the human to comprehend that which lies beyond the human – but which, as beyond the human, may still be invested with being, order, and meaning. This in turn leads to a derivative knowing of this unknowing. And here, darkness indicates the conciliatory ability to comprehend the incomprehensibility of what remains, outside the human.

Then there is, secondly, the limit of that which cannot be known by us, the limit of the limit, as it were. With the limit of human knowing, there is still the presupposition of something outside that is simply a limit for us as human beings. The limit of the limit is not a constraint or boundary, but a "darkening" of the principle of sufficient divinity. It suggests that there is nothing outside, and that this nothing-outside is absolutely inaccessible. This leads not to a conciliatory knowing of unknowing, which is really a knowing of something that cannot be known. Instead, it is a negative knowing of nothing to know. *There is nothing, and it cannot be known.*

We've been tracing the motif of darkness in mystical texts, and the way in which the concept of darkness is often compounded, duplicitous, and enigmatic. Each of our examples stems from the Dionysian tradition of negative theology, or the *via negativa*. Each puts forth a concept of negation that is tied in some way to the motif of darkness, though darkness is not always negative for each of these thinkers. And each example reaches its limit in a concept of the divine that we have been "mis-reading" in terms of the horror of philosophy – the limits of the human, the unreliable knowledge of such limits, the human confronting something it can only name as *unhuman*. Such a darkness is not in any way an answer, much less a solution, to some of the issues we face today concerning climate change, posthumanism, or what Bataille once called "the congested planet." In a way, thinking this type of darkness is doomed to failure, devolving as it does on its own limits.

And, perhaps, the greatest lesson from all this is the one repeatedly stated by Eckhart – that this darkness, in its unknowing, is not separate from us, but really within us as well. It is not a darkness "out there" in the great beyond, but an "outside" (to use Bataille's term) that is co-extensive with the human at its absolute limit. It runs the gamut from the lowest to the highest, from the self to the planet, from the human to the unhuman. It is a sentiment echoed by Bataille when he speaks about darkness as a form of impossibility:

> enter into a dead end. There all possibilities are exhausted; the "possible" slips away and the impossible prevails. To face the impossible – exorbitant, indubitable – when nothing is possible any longer is in my eyes to have an experience of the divine...[55]

* * *

Blanchot's Night. Although the concept of darkness can be parsed and analyzed in a variety of ways, at its core is a duplicity: darkness as absence, and darkness as the presence of absence. This is a duplicity that marks many of the mystical texts on darkness, from Dionysius to Meister Eckhart on down to modern authors such as Georges Bataille and Maurice Blanchot.

Blanchot's short text from 1955, "The Outside, the Night," encapsulates this dual aspect of darkness in his characteristically lyrical, philosophical language: "In the night, everything has disappeared. This is the first night. Here absence approaches – silence, repose, night... Here language completes and fulfills itself in the silent profundity which vouches for it as its meaning."[56] This is night as indelibly tied to day, "another of day's constructions," nocturnal sleep opposed to daytime labor, nighttime dream opposed to daytime reality, oblivion opposed to the incessant production of meaning. In this night poets wander among nocturnal graveyards, gothic protagonists confuse moonlit illusion and reality, and a whole bestiary of impossible beings seems suddenly probable. This is the lyrical night evoked by Edward Young's *Night Thoughts*, by Charles Baudelaire's elegies to the moon, by Novalis' *Hymns to the Night*: "Away I turn to the holy, the unspeakable, the secretive Night. Down over there, far, lies the world – sunken in a deep vault – its place wasted and lonely. In the heart's strings, deep sadness blows. In dewdrops I'll sink and mix with the ashes."[57]

This first night is inseparable – but distinct from – another kind of night, which Blanchot simply refers to as "the other night." In the first night, everything has disappeared. "But when everything has disappeared in the night, 'everything has disappeared' appears. This is the *other* night."[58] Whereas the first night is the night of dichotomies (night/day, dusk/dawn, darkness/light), this other night is more austere, the mere registering of absence, of disappearance, of negation. "Night is this apparition: 'everything has disappeared.'"[59] This other night is the night of phantoms, specters, apparitions, visions, and haunting. But, Blanchot notes, "this eeriness does not simply come from something invisible, which would reveal itself under cover of dark and at the shadows' summons." That is because all these dreams, illusions, and apparitions are merely phenomena which serve as fragile, tenuous veils of a kind of non-phenomena, an absence that is, at the same time, "there." Night is the phenomena of the absence of phenomena. "Here the invisible is what cannot cease to see; it is the incessant making itself seen." Blanchot's most concise formulation: "What appears in the night is the night that appears."

This dichotomy of the two kinds of night is found not only in Blanchot's philosophy but in his fictional works as well. His short novel *Thomas the Obscure* is an extended meditation on this "other night" as it gradually seeps into, or emerges from, the titular character. From a philosophical perspective, what Blanchot is trying to do is to think about "night" in a way that is not simply the opposite of day – that is, a concept of night that is not simply privative. This parallels the examples from the history of Western mysticism, in which, as Dionysius the Areopagite notes, there is a kind of "darkness" beyond the privative darkness opposed to light.

Whether Blanchot as a writer succeeds in doing this, is an open question. The more important issue that arises from his short essay is whether "philosophy" resides on the side of day or the side of night. And if on the side of night, which night is it: the romantic, lyrical night, or this "other" night? In so far as philosophy is dedicated to constructing concepts, argument, and systems of knowledge, it would seem to be a "daytime" activity. Yet every philosophy harbors within it elements that undermine it – contradiction, paradox, inconsistency, vagueness, lack of direction or goal. Blanchot seems readily aware of the various tactics which "daytime" philosophical thought employs to both acknowledge the nocturnal element while keeping it separate from the daytime labors of philosophy. There is, Blanchot notes, a classical tactic, associated with Greek philosophy, one of balance and moderation, night as a limit that must not be transgressed. Then there's an Enlightenment tactic, in which night is by definition what the daytime work of philosophy's empire must dissolve and dissipate, the light of reason exploding into the darkness of ignorance. And finally, there's a modern tactic, in which daytime philosophy aims not just to dissolve, but to absorb and sublimate night, to make use of it in an ongoing engine of progressive, dialectical reason, ascending to higher and higher planes of knowledge-production.

And yet, Blanchot remains committed to this "other night." He does not say that it is totally outside of language or thought; but neither does he give it any positive, concrete determination. Blanchot's enigmatic novel *Thomas the Obscure* captures this "other night" in its detailed yet obscure depictions of Thomas' morose inner states. In it, the most innocuous of situations, such as walking home at dusk, reveals a whole unexpected universe of nocturnal affects:

The night was more somber and more painful than he could have expected. The darkness immersed everything; there was no hope of passing through its shadows, but one penetrated its reality in a relationship of overwhelming intimacy. His first observation was that he could still use his body, and particularly his eyes; it was not that he saw anything, but what he looked at eventually placed him in contact with a nocturnal mass which he vaguely perceived to be himself and in which he was bathed... for him, it was as if fear had immediately conquered him, and it was with a sense of shame that he raised his head to accept the idea he had entertained: outside himself there was something identical to his own thought which his glance or his hand could touch. Repulsive fantasy. Soon the night seemed to him gloomier and more terrible than any night, as if it had in fact issued from a wound of thought which had ceased to think... It was night itself.[60]

This other night is "outside" only in so far as its very conception (as "other night") takes place within the familiar light of philosophy's day. We are all daylight philosophers, especially those of us – Blanchot included – enamored of the night. "Only in the day does it [the other night] seem comprehensible, ascertainable. In the day it is the secret which could be disclosed; it is something concealed that awaits its unveiling. Only the day can feel passion for the night."[61] In this way Blanchot's ruminations on the futility of philosophy, of thinking this other night, result in an itinerary – but an itinerary of futility. "One must live in the day and labor for its sake. Yes, one has to do that. But to labor for the day is to find, in the end, the night; it is thus to make night the job of the day, to make night a task and an abode."[62]

This itinerary is a peculiar one, for it ends not with philosophy's conquest of its object, but the reverse – the inessential, the impossible, the futile. One can sense this looking back from Blanchot's text to authors such as Dionysius, Angela of Foligno, and John of the Cross. Blanchot's philosophical search for night is at once an impossibility and an itinerary. It also characterizes contemporary poetic meditations on the topic, such as the pseudonymous text *Songs from the Black Moon*, authored by one Rasu-Yong Tugen. Employing much of the language of the darkness-mysticism tradition, it emphasizes this turn towards the futility of thought, while at the same time evoking Blanchot's night:

> In eternal night,
> we had each burned the forest
> in order to better see.
>
> Clouds of sorrowful ravens
> drifted upwards,
> imperceptibly blotting out the stars.[63]

Another pseudonymous collection, *Cantos for the Crestfallen*, by an author known as Pseudo-Leopardi, puts it in equally stark terms:

> Cease to imagine my intelligibility to you, stop trying
> To exit the darkness, the vast unilluminable melody
> Of night shrouding the corpse of this world from view.[64]

If this other night has any value for Blanchot, it is not because it points to some other, better place, above or beyond the tired dichotomy of day/night, but because the other night is always something that one fails to adequately think. It is philosophy fascinated by a line of thought that culminates in its own silence: "Whoever sense the approach of the *other* night has the impression that he is approaching the heart of the night, the essential night which he seeks. And no doubt it is 'at this moment' that he gives himself up to the inessential and loses all possibility."[65]

* * *

The Black Universe. Some time ago I was doing research for a seminar I planned to offer on "media and magic." I was interested in the concept of magic as it existed in the Renaissance, and in particular with the so-called occult philosophy of thinkers like Marsilio Ficino, Giordano Bruno, Heinrich Cornelius Agrippa, and Robert Fludd. It was while reading about Fludd that I discovered a startling image. It was from his major work, an ambitious, multi-volume, syncretic theory-of-everything with the cumbersome title *The Metaphysical, Physical, and Technical History of the Two Worlds, the Major as well as the Minor.* Fludd published his work between 1617 and 1621, and each volume is generously supplied with diagrams, tables, and images. The image that jumped out at me is quite simple. In a section discussing the origin of the universe, Fludd was compelled to speculate on what existed prior to the universe, which he describes as an empty nothingness, a sort of "pre-universe" or "un-universe." He chose to represent this with a simple black square.

The image was startling to me because it was so different from the other images of Fludd's that we are used to – elaborate, ornate, hyper-complex diagrams that detail all the movements of the planets or of the mind. The black square was also startling because it immediately brought to mind examples from modern art, the most noteworthy being Kazimir Malevich's *Black Square on a White Ground* from 1915. Being a former literature student, I was also reminded of the enigmatic "black page" from Lawrence Sterne's *The Life and Opinions of Tristram Shandy, Gentleman* (1759-67). Fludd's black square was, to be sure, enigmatic. Not only that, but Fludd also seemed aware of the limits of representation, noting, on each edge of the black square, *Et sic in infinitum*, "And so on to infinity…"

Looking at it out of context, I find Fludd's image indelibly modern, both in its simplicity and its austerity. It was as if Fludd had the intuition that only a self-negating form of representation would be able to suggest the nothingness prior to all existence, an un-creation prior to all creation. And so we get a "color" that is not really a color – a color that either negates or consumes all colors. And we get a square that is not really a square, a box meant to indicate boundlessness. For the image to work within the context of Fludd's cosmology, the viewer must *not* see the image for what it is – a black square. The viewer must understand the square as formlessness, and the black inside as neither a fullness nor an emptiness. This simple little image requires a lot of work on the part of the viewer, perhaps as much work as in Fludd's other, more complex diagrams. For a synthetic, systematic thinker like Fludd, this must have been a difficult move. After all, *The Metaphysical, Physical, and Technical History…* is, if nothing else, a totalizing work, and work whose ambition is to include and to account for everything – even nothing.

That Fludd would choose to do this is not surprising. His own syncretic philosophy combined elements of Neoplatonism, hermeticism, and Christian Kabbalah, with a touch of alchemy, music theory, Renaissance mechanics, and Rosicrucianism. Trained as a physician, Fludd was influenced early on by the work of Paracelsus, and was intrigued by the idea of God as an alchemist, mixing matter to produce the strange brew that is the universe. At one point, Fludd describes the state prior to creation as "the mist and darkness of this hitherto shapeless and obscured region," in which the "impure, dark, and dense part of the abyss' substance" is dramatically transformed by divine light.[66] The black square is quickly followed by a series of images – almost like a stop-motion animation – in which the divine *fiat* of creation and light flows forth. The Neoplatonic theme of the divine as a central source of radiating light takes over, producing the macrocosm and the microcosm, the ethereal and the earthly domains, all the stuff of the world.

I lose interest in much of what follows, detailed and systematic though it is. But I continue to find the black square fascinating because of the contradictions in it. An image that, in order to be seen, negates itself. An un-universe that can only present its own absence. A boundless abyss that gives itself forth in an infinite austerity. Of course, words fail. For every un-universe, then, an un-philosophy that must also negate itself.

* * *

Dark, Black. But here we should remind ourselves that black is not just dark, but, well, black. If darkness implies a shrouding, a tenebrous obfuscation, should we then say that blackness is a blotting-out, a nullification of every existent? If darkness both "is" and "is not," is this also the case with blackness?

In his discussion of the crucifixion, Nicola Masciandaro shows us a moment in which darkness becomes blackness. His takeoff point is the interim of uncertainty, confusion, and anguish when Christ, on the cross, cries out "My God, my God, why has thou forsaken me?" The Gospels describe this interim period as one of a profound, even universal darkness: "Now from the sixth hour there was darkness over all the land until the ninth hour"; "It was now about the sixth hour, and there was darkness over the whole land until the ninth hour, while the sun's light failed."[67] In one traditional reading of this passage, Christ's cries of sorrowful doubt are not just the cries of one individual, but, allegorically, of every individual. In this breach between an anguished self and a seemingly indifferent cosmos, something appears. What appears is this breach, this fracture or lacuna at the core of existence. What appears is this "darkness"; what appears is precisely what one cannot see, and what one apprehends is, in anguish, that one cannot apprehend. Masciandaro: "It becomes a strange place where the only way to discern where you are with certainty is to see that you are hopelessly lost."[68] Masciandaro names this enigmatic breach "sorrow."

It is in this breach, this sorrow, that Masciandaro suggests an even more radical reading of this "crucifixion darkness." Beyond the suffering of Christ on the cross, and beyond the allegorical suffering of all individuals vis-à-vis a world that seems indifferent to them, there is a sorrow that is not simply that of individual human subjects that feel emotions. For Masciandaro the real lesson of crucifixion darkness is that sorrow is, in a way, exterior to the human being: "it is the image of a cosmos that cries, the image of tears that are materially at the heart of its being made."[69] It is here that darkness becomes blackness. For, "the universe itself, an entity that most certainly includes your being in it, and vice-versa, is... the dark realm of a literally authentic melancholy, that is, sorrow humorially proper to *black earth*."[70]

In this philosophical, or rather, mystical sense, black is less a color and more the withdrawal of every relation between self and world, resulting in this breach which, nevertheless, makes itself apparent as such. The sorrow that results is not simply the forlorn sorrow of finite, emotive human beings, but something impersonal and withering in existence itself. "There rests the difference between black and darkness," Masciandaro notes. "Darkness is a property of black, but black is not darkness. Shadow, nothingness, void look black and black is something *before* shadow, nothingness, void..."[71] If, in this formulation, darkness always exists in some relation to light, however gradated, tenebrous, and shadowy, then blackness is something anterior to both light and dark. François Laruelle encapsulates this in one of his early, experimental texts, "Du noir univers": "Black is anterior to the absence of light, whether this absence be the shadows that extinguish it, whether it be its nothingness or its positive opposite."[72] Masciandaro extends this: "It is true that black is what is seen in the absence of light. But black is not that absence. Black is its own presence, not the presence of the absence of light."[73] Color and cosmos become intertwined in this blackness, something that neither exists nor does not exist; it's "is" is precisely it's "is not."

* * *

Nothing to See. Color and cosmos also intertwine in Fludd's black square. And the use of black in his cosmology is indicative of what modern color theory has had to say about black. On the one hand, black is not considered to be a color in the conventional sense of the term. Black objects are those that do not reflect light in the visible spectrum; thus color theory refers to black as "non-chromatic" or "achromatic." A further nuance is the notion that black is the condition without any light – largely a theoretical proposition, or at least one that would have to be verified without being seen. But already there is some ambiguity, for does black designate a "color" that does not reflect light (and if so, why label it a color?), or does black designate the "color" that results in the total absence of light? Without light, no color, and without color, there is only black – and yet black is not a color. But this is not exactly right, for black is a color, not only in the sense in which we routinely designate this or that object as "black" but in the sense that black contains all colors, the color that absorbs all other colors into the non-color of black – the black hole of color, as it were. We see black, but what exactly are we seeing when we see black? – light, or the absence of light? And if the latter, how is it possible to see the absence of light?

While black as a color has a rich and varied history in terms of its symbolic meanings, it would take a modern, scientific theory of color to begin to address such questions. When Goethe published his *Color Theory* in 1810, such conundrums were largely ignored in aesthetics, and often not discussed in the science of optics. But Goethe, being the polymath that he was, was not content to write a treatise of aesthetics. The *Color Theory* is as much a science of color as it is an aesthetics; indeed, the aim is to attempt the synthesis of the two. Goethe's major contribution was to distinguish the "visible" from the "optical" spectrum, and to make possible a science of optics that would be distinct from that of aesthetics, but which would overlap with it as well.[74] Goethe's project is determined to consider color as a physiological phenomenon, to "search for nothing beyond the phenomena" of seeing color through the apparatus of the eye. For Goethe, any theory of color must begin from the physiological event of seeing color.

But black proves to be a difficult color to discuss for Goethe. In the opening sections of his treatise, "black" is often interchangeable with "dark" and "shadow," all three terms denoting a physiological state when the eye is deprived of light: "If we keep the eyes open in a totally dark place, a certain sense of privation is experienced. The organ is abandoned to itself; it retires into itself. That stimulating and grateful contact is wanting by means of which it is connected with the external world…"[75] Black is conceived of in privative terms, in terms of the absence of light – not unlike Fludd's cosmic black square.

And, black is even moralized by Goethe (as it is in Fludd), for the light that enables sight is not just a physiological stimulation, but a quasi-divine gift. When Goethe does briefly discuss black later on in his treatise, it is largely to discuss the combustion and oxidation processes that produce blackness in objects such as wood or metal. Strangely, Goethe does not raise the problem of black as a color, choosing instead to analyze the chemical process of blackening, and in the process sounding very much like a Renaissance alchemist.

Goethe's *Color Theory* had an immediate impact on the philosophy and science of color. One person particularly taken by it was Arthur Schopenhauer, who knew Goethe and discussed color theory with him on several occasions. While Schopenhauer does not depart from Goethe's distinction between the visible and the optical, he does attempt to root color theory in philosophy more than science. Schopenhauer's *On Vision and Colors* was published in 1816, just three years after the completion of his doctoral dissertation. A short book, it does not display the systematicity of *The World as Will and Representation* nor the aphoristic pessimism of his late writings. What it does do is drive a wedge into Goethe's *Color Theory*. Goethe, Schopenhauer claimed, does not really present a theory of color, foremost because he never considers what color is – that color exists is something assumed in his treatise.

Furthermore, Schopenhauer took Goethe to task for another assumption – that the perception of color necessarily corresponded to color itself, as if it were a physical thing in itself. Being a good Kantian, Schopenhauer tended to understand color as a cognitive process that began with the sensation of light and resulted in the cognitive representation of color. Schopenhauer was even more precise in identifying the "intensive activity of the retina" as the main apparatus for the perception of color. The trick was to understand what it was that made an impression on the retina in the first place; was color something identifiable in the world as such (i.e. as light), or was it merely a by-product of the physiology of vision?[76] Where did color take place? To say that we receive light that stimulates our retina is one thing, but to show how color is necessarily produced from this activity is quite another. In Schopenhauer's theory of perception, the theory of color begins to ever so slightly slip away – and yet, he admits, some vague entity called "color" could be identified, classified, measured, even agreed upon in an everyday context.

As with Goethe, for Schopenhauer the problem is black, which he sees as inseparable from white. Black and white are strange entities in Schopenhauer's treatise. At some points they seem to be additions or privations of light, much in line with Goethe: "The influence of light and white on the retina and its ensuing activity have degrees according to which light steadily approaches darkness and white approaches black."[77] But at other points black and white function more as logical necessities, forming the absolute poles of color perception; that is, black and white are never actually seen, and yet they determine the perception of color.[78] And, later in the treatise, there is even a third, more naturalistic interpretation, one that has to do specifically with black and not with white: that black is simply the physiological state of "retinal inactivity."[79] The eye without sight – or without vision.

After all is said and done, Schopenhauer's questions prove to be more interesting than his answers. All the same, it is tempting to make some connections between Schopenhauer's color theory and his pessimistic philosophy. A central ambiguity of Schopenhauer's *On Vision and Colors* has to do with black. Is black something that can be seen, like any other color? Or is black simply the name for something in the structure of vision that conditions color perception – but which can never be seen in itself? Perhaps there is a black that is seen – the black of shading and gradients – as well as a black that is unseen – the black of retinal inactivity. And here again we seem to return to the paradox of Fludd's black square – the black that can only be seen at the expense of ceasing to be black (where black becomes "dark" or "shade"). Perhaps – and here we're being generous to Schopenhauer's text – there is a *retinal pessimism* that secretly underlies color theory, encapsulated in the notion of black as privation (Goethe), black as retinal inactivity (Schopenhauer), black as that which precedes the very existence of light itself (Fludd). Retinal pessimism is not simply the failure of the phenomena of perception, the physiology of the retina, or the science of optics. Nor is it the conviction that whatever one is seeing is the worst of all possible things that could be seen. Both are intriguing options. But, retinal pessimism is something else, and it is encapsulated in the strange status of black: at once present and absent, at once a fullness and an emptiness, at once the absorption of all light and the total absence of light. Black is at once the foundation of all color and, in its absence or emptiness, it is also what undermines the substantiality of all color. If one is willing to go down this path, retinal pessimism is not just about the non-color that is black, but it is about the perception of color itself. It is, ultimately, the suspicion that *all* colors are black, that *all* retinal activity is retinal inactivity. Retinal pessimism: there is nothing to see (and you're seeing it).

* * *

Black on Black. The question is, what would such a retinal pessimism see, if it is not simply the physiological state of blindness, or the metaphorical state of "inner vision"? Not surprisingly, artists have thought about this question, and there is, of course, a history of black painting in modern art.[80] For me the most notable example is that of Ad Reinhardt, who, in the 1960s, produced a number of paintings that, at first glance, appear to be all matte black, much in the tradition of Malevich. But after looking at the painting for some time, what appears to be black is not black at all. Instead, subtle hues of deep mauve, purple, magenta, and gray become apparent. And the uniform black canvas reveals a grid, or a series of squares within the canvas, each of a slightly different color. The painting actually changes within the duration of its viewing. "Black" literally vanishes as one looks at it, and what quietly emerges are colors and shapes. Reinhardt's paintings are almost visual analogues for Fludd's cosmology.

But modern black painting is, in a way, too predictable a place to begin, for black paintings always push black up front, in front of the viewer, as something to be seen. My own fascination with black in painting comes not from abstract expressionism, but from an earlier period – the infinite, stark, black backgrounds in Velázquez's "The Water Seller of Seville" (1618-22), the black clouds that envelop Rembrandt's "The Abduction of Proserpine" (1631), the almost Surreal flatness of Zurburan's "Christ on the Cross" (1627). As a painter of black, the artist that stands out from the rest for me is Caravaggio. In fact, I only came to appreciate modern black painting in seeing paintings like "The Crucifixion of St. Peter" (1601), "St. Matthew and the Angel" (1602), and "David with the Head of Goliath" (1605; 1609/10). One painting in particular I never tire of, and that is Caravaggio's "St. Jerome Writing" (c.1606).

Certainly in paintings like this Caravaggio makes extreme use of chiaroscuro, and he is not the first to do so. But there is a sense that Caravaggio took as much care painting the black backgrounds as he did the lighted figures in the foreground. Caravaggio's black is ambiguous. In one part of the canvas the black background is flat and full. In another part it is an empty, infinite depth. In still another part it is a thick black cloud, miasmatically embracing the foreground figures. The wonderful echo between the saint's barely haloed head and the skull holding open the book is accentuated by one kind of black – a black of shadows, shading, and contour. But behind both skull and head there is only outer space, at once flat and infinite. In a strange optical illusion, this same cosmic black seems to also inhabit the edges of the books, the space underneath the table, the creases of the fabric, and Jerome's own wrists. For me, this is "black painting" – black as a background that is always about to eclipse the foreground, the groundlessness of the figure/ground distinction itself, the presence of an absence, a retinal pessimism.

Black painting – of the abstract expressionist type – has had a long career in modern art. And a survey of contemporary art suggests that black is always back, in some shape or form. But what I find interesting about black artworks today is the way they seem to combine the likes of abstract expressionism with that of Caravaggio and his tenebrist contemporaries. An example is Terence Hannum's series "Veils" (2012), which consists of images of disembodied hair on a black background – St. Jerome as a headbanger, as it were.

The wisps of hair not only recall the black drawings of abstract expressionism, but they give the same sense of flat depth evoked in Caravaggio, in which we see figures almost drowning in black. Black is not only flat background, but a background that literally engulfs the foreground figure into a seemingly infinite abyss below, above, behind, everywhere.

A further play on the foreground/background distinction

comes in Jonah Groeneboer's drawings, which often feature luminous, geometric forms against a cloudy black background. In a different vein, Juliet Jacobson's series of black drawings, with their dense, thick, pulverizing of graphite on paper, pick up a different aspect of Fludd and the occult philosophers – that of their material, chemical, and alchemical commitment to the connection between the microcosm and macrocosm. And it is worth noting that each of these contemporary artists produces their black artworks through very material, physical processes that are also processes of negation: rubbing, smearing, smudging, and erasing material like graphite or charcoal into shards of powder and dust. The process seems adequate for the result, the showing of nothing, the revealing of black less as a color and more as this "nothing-to-see."

It is this transition – from black as a color you see, to black as a non-color you don't see, to black as "nothing-to-see" (and you're seeing it) – that Fludd encapsulates in his simple black square. For Fludd, black was the "color" of non-existence, of pre-existence, of an un-universe prior to its possibility. This idea has also come full circle in contemporary philosophy. In a short and opaque text entitled "On the Black Universe," the French thinker François Laruelle extends this idea of black as a cosmological principle. Neither an aesthetics of color nor a metaphor for knowledge and ignorance, black is, for Laruelle, inseparable from the conditions of thought and its limit. Separate from "the World" we make in our own, all-too-human image, and apart from "the Earth" which tolerates our habitation of its surface, there is "the Universe" – indifferent, opaque, black: "Black prior to light is the substance of the Universe, what escaped from the World before the World was born into the World."[81]

In such a scenario, human beings probe the Earth and manufacture the World, but neither of these respond to the groping around that constitutes being, or being-there, or becoming-this-or-that, or the event, or what have you. The human being "is answered only by the Universe, being black and mute."[82] And yet, it is this enigmatic response that leads us into thinking that this black universe, the black of Fludd's un-universe, is something "out there" – the nature of reality, the fabric of the universe, a consensual hallucination, something that I can see and touch and feel, a color. Laruelle again: "A phenomenal blackness entirely fills the essence of the human.

Because of it, the most ancient stars of the paleo-cosmos, together with the most venerable stones of the archeo-earth, appear to the human as being outside the World..."[83] Fludd's cosmic black square, his un-universe, is not temporally prior to the universe, but neither is it some cataclysm to come; it is right here. But you can't see it. (And you're seeing it.)

Black is the color of ink, oil, crows, mourning, and outer space. Black is not just one color among others, and neither is it one element or material among others. Black bathes all things in an absence, makes apparent an opacity, evaporates all the nuances of shadow and light. I leave the last word to an alchemist of a different sort, Yohji Yamamoto, who provides yet another variation of black: "...Above all, black says this: I don't bother you – don't bother me."

3

Prayers for Nothing

Horror Vacui. Philosophy in the West has, for some time, been haunted by the idea of non-being. The earliest Greek philosophers we know of differed widely in their ideas about the nature of reality, some arguing that everything was composed of water (Thales), or air (Anaximenes), or fire (Heraclitus), or miniscule moving atoms (Democritus). Others offered more conceptual notions, that of reality being composed of a universal mind (Anaxagoras' *nous*), of a principle of boundlessness (Anaximander's *aperion*), of a numerical principle (Pythagoras), or a principle of unity or oneness (Parmenides).

As different as these philosophies are, they are united in their commitment to the idea that there *is* something. The task for the philosopher is thus to determine what that something is – or better, what the "is" is. One both assumes that there is something at all, and that this something that "is" is all there is. There is something, and beyond that – there is nothing. But this assumes a great deal, for every assertion of something fundamental of reality that "is" there is an automatic counter-assertion of something else that "is not." When Heraclitus argues that reality is composed of "fire" (as dynamic and always-changing) he is implicitly arguing that there is something that is not-fire (that is static, unchanging, immobile). But more than that, the philosopher, in making such arguments on the nature of reality, must assume that there is something at all about which one can make arguments. It may be that we are fooled by our senses, or have grown used to certain ways of thinking, or that we simply cannot – or will not – entertain the idea that there is nothing. In this sense, it matters little whether the nature of reality is water, fire, air, or mind – what must be addressed in all these theories is that there "is" something at all.

Hence the central question that has, in one way or another, come to occupy Western metaphysics: why is there something rather than nothing? The stakes are high if one chooses to address such a question. Aristotle understood this early on, which is why his approach is not to offer yet another theory-of-everything, but to step back and analyze the question.[84] He begins to chip away at the problem, distinguishing three questions that occupy metaphysical speculation: first, the question of whether there "is" something; second, if there is something, the question of whether we can know this something; and third, if we can know this something, the question of how we can clearly articulate it in language. All this proceeds from that first question – that there is something rather than nothing. Without this first assertion, this foundation, everything else crumbles. But how can there be nothing – how can we say that nothing "is"?

Aristotle is characteristically cautious in his analysis. He summarizes the different views on what he terms the "void" or "vacuum," and finds that many of the views assume the void to be defined in terms of empty space. Ambiguity ensues, as philosophers attempt to render the nothing as something; the void is not the container itself, but the nothing that "is" in the container, at best negatively demonstrated by displaced space (e.g. water poured into an empty vessel). In this "plenist" view, the void is simply that which is not-yet-full, or that which is not-X, where X denotes an existent, actual body, and the void simply the interval or relation between one body and another, the space in-between. Hence the well-known statement often attributed to Aristotle: that nature abhors a vacuum. In these and other views that Aristotle summarizes, the void seems to always slip away from thought, at once something that exists and that, by definition, cannot exist – both "is" and "is not." Aristotle concludes, "if there is a void, a result follows which is the very opposite of the reason for which those who believe in a void set it up."[85]

Aristotle's analysis is helpful because it distinguishes two aspects of the idea of non-being: (i) a metaphysical aspect, in which one thinks about non-being as empty or full, an entity or a relation; and (ii) a logical aspect, in which one deals with what it means to state that non-being "is." For the moment we will be clustering terms together – non-being, nothing, and nothingness. But very quickly we will see that they will take on different meanings. Again, for Aristotle as for other philosophers, the stakes of such speculations are significant. The question "why is there something rather than nothing?" could quite possibly result in the response "there is nothing." And if there is nothing, then not only is philosophy's endeavor futile, but it is also absurd. Here is where the "horror of philosophy" comes into play. This is the thought that philosophy cannot think without undermining itself. To say "there is nothing" is to evoke silence, or at least to render philosophical discourse absurd. It is a limit to thought, and in particular, to the humanist preoccupation with thinking everything (including... nothing). Granted, while the possible reply "there is nothing" does not prevent philosophy from continuing – if anything, philosophy finds a new task, which is to state, with all the contradiction it implies, "there is nothing" – the reply "there is nothing" prompts us to question some fundamental premises of both the philosophical project and philosophical thought.

Our trajectory will be highly eclectic, though methodical. After a consideration of the question "why is there something rather than nothing" in modern philosophy, we will examine the concept of nothing (*niht*) in the work of Meister Eckhart, who offers a multi-faceted concept of nothing that also encompasses its contradictions, before then turning to the Japanese philosophers associated with the Kyoto School, and their own development of the concept of *śūnyatā* or "emptiness."

* * *

Nothing and Nothingness (Heidegger, Sartre, Badiou). One of the insights of Heidegger's *Being and Time* is that the question of being in and of itself can be distinguished – but not separated from – the question of this or that particular being or entity. As he notes, "the question which we are to work out, what is asked about is Being – that which determines entities as entities, that on the basis of which entities are already understood… The Being of entities 'is' not itself an entity."[86] For any philosophy which aims to examine being as such, this "ontological difference" between Being and entities is the first step. One may ask about the being of this or that particular entity, but this is still asking about *beings* rather than *Being*. Heidegger's tongue-twisting terminology "the Being of beings" encapsulates this distinction. Being is not one being among other beings, but that which is common to all beings. This means that Being can be examined, but only obliquely, via beings, and for Heidegger it is the being specific to human beings that provides this privileged vantage point. Human being is unique for Heidegger because it is the being for whom Being is an issue, a particular type of being "thrown" into the particularity of this world but orienting itself towards being in general – it is a type of being Heidegger famously terms *Dasein* (literally, "being-there").

In this sort of inquiry, asking about Being also means asking about what Being is not; one says there is Being, and beyond that, nothing. It is a grand, totalizing inquiry that at once encompasses everything and also says that, by virtue of its totality, there is nothing else to consider. To do so would be futile. To paraphrase Heidegger, the Being of beings is not itself a being. This would seem tantamount to saying that Being is, literally, "nothing." Heidegger addresses this in his lecture "What is Metaphysics?" where merely posing the question reveals all sorts of dizzying conundrums:

...we shall try to ask about the nothing. What is the nothing? Our very first approach to this question has something unusual about it. In our asking we posit the nothing in advance as something that "is" such and such; we posit it as a being. But that is exactly what it is distinguished from. Interrogating the nothing – asking what and how it, the nothing, is – turns what is interrogated into its opposite. The question deprives itself of its own object.[87]

As Heidegger notes, the question itself cannot be posed without immediately falling into contradiction. Being – as that which is the ground and held in common among all beings – this Being is not itself a being, and thus is also non-being. And it is this contra-diction that leads him to parse out two types of "nothing": first, a nothing viewed in terms of opposition to beings, as their negation, and secondly, a nothing that is identical with Being (in so far as Being is not a being). Heidegger briefly comments on the concept of nothing in classical Greek and medieval Christian philosophy, before offering this distinction:

This cursory historical review shows the nothing as the counter-concept to being proper, that is, as its negation. But if the nothing becomes any problem at all, then... it awakens for the first time the proper formulation of the metaphysical question concerning the Being of beings. The nothing does not remain the indeterminate opposite of beings but reveals itself as belonging to the Being of beings.[88]

For Heidegger, "nothing" names this paradoxical quality of Being, as everywhere and nowhere, as held in common among beings but never present in and of itself. The upshot of all this is that moment when the human being apprehends this "nothing" in the confrontation with one's own mortality. It is in confronting the "indefiniteness of death" that the human being holds itself out over an abyss, and for a brief, fleeting moment, glimpses the Being of beings as "nothing." The being specific to the human being is "held out into the nothing." This existential state Heidegger famously terms *Angst* (anxiety, dread): "The indefiniteness of death is primordially disclosed in anxiety... The 'nothing' with which anxiety brings us face to face, unveils the nullity by which Dasein, in its vary basis, is defined; and this basis itself is thrownness into death."[89]

Dramatic though it sounds, this confrontation with nothing is for Heidegger both the height and the depth of the human being. As Heidegger shows in his analyses of everyday moods such as boredom and anxiety, more often than not we shun "the nothing" in favor of immersion in the purely affirmative world of our individuated beings. This is Jean-Paul Sartre's takeoff point in the first part of *Being and Nothingness*. There Sartre begins from the situation of beings – in particular, human beings – alienated from their own being; in Heidegger's terms, we are beings shut off from Being. But Sartre is more concerned with the human being's relation to being in itself. It is in this relation that generates what Sartre terms "nothingness" (*le néant*). For Sartre, when the human being asks about being as such, nothingness reveals itself in several ways: as an indetermination on the side of the questioner, on the side of that which is questioned, and in the possibility of there not being any meaning to the questioning itself. "The permanent possibility of non-being, outside us and within, conditions our questions about being."[90] The human being attempts to manage all these uncertainties by fixing its object of inquiry: "Being is *that* and outside of that, *nothing*."[91]

For Sartre, "nothingness" is the moment when the "outside of that, nothing" creeps back into the concern with being. Sartre gives the everyday example of going to a café to meet someone. Let's say I am going to Joe Coffee to meet Prema. I enter the café, expecting to find her, but she isn't there. I scan the café, the people sitting or standing, the tables and chairs, the counter with the tattooed baristas, and I hear the clanking of espresso cups, coffee grinder, and dimly-audible music in the background. But this is all a backdrop to Prema, who I expect to find, and who isn't there. I may shift my attention to foreground elements in the café (do they really need to take up that much space with their laptop?, those two students over there are talking way too loud, I should buy some coffee beans while I'm here, and oh, there's Dominic over there, hi…). But this does not efface the basic differential between the background (Joe Coffee) and an absent foreground (Prema). I have, in Sartre's terms, "nihilated" the café as background, to make way for the expected foreground of Prema – who is not there. A kind of abyss opens up, a presence of an absence. It is Prema's raising herself up as nothingness against the nihilated backdrop that is the café. As Sartre notes, "what is offered to intuition is a flickering of nothingness; it is the nothingness of the ground, the nihilation of which summons and demands the appearance of the figure."[92]

What this means is that Sartre's notion of nothingness is nearly the opposite of that of Heidegger. For Heidegger "the nothing" is consummate with Being, which is itself not one being among others, and which also has a philosophical priority over this or that being. But for Sartre, the example of the café reveals that there is always first a being that is then "not there" – there is always first an "is" that is secondarily "not": "This means that being is prior to nothingness and establishes the ground for it. By this we must understand not only that being has a logical precedence over nothingness but also that it is from being that nothingness derives concretely its efficacy."[93] This is crucial for Sartre as it will allow him to argue for a notion of "freedom" based on this loosening between intention and act, between expecting someone and not finding them there. It will serve as the basis for his famous dictum "existence precedes essence."

In spite of their differences, what both Heidegger and Sartre grapple with is the enigma of nothing/nothingness for philosophy, an enigma that asks philosophy to think, in a single thought, the "is" and "is not" of nothing/nothingness. Heidegger cloaks the nothing with the language of Being and beings, in which "the nothing" is not that which opposes Being but which is fully commensurate with it. Sartre similarly cloaks nothingness with a different language, that of an encounter between beings and the rift that may result when an expected encounter does not take place. Should we say that, for Heidegger, "the nothing" is an absent presence, and for Sartre, "nothingness" is a present absence? Perhaps this is simplifying things too much.

Alain Badiou adds another wrinkle to the discussion. Employing elements of mathematical set theory, Badiou uses the term "void" to designate the combined "is" and "is not" with which Heidegger and Sartre grapple. Badiou's terminology is highly technical, but, simplifying to the extreme, we might say that, for Badiou, the void captures both Heidegger's link between the nothing and Being, and Sartre's concept of nothingness that is set against the backdrop of beings. If we think of set theory in terms of classification systems, those boxes (or "sets") into which we place different things (or "elements"), then the void (or "empty set") is that set that has no elements (the box with nothing in it). And yet, it still can be designated as an empty set (with the double bracket {} or the symbol Ø). Thus the empty set designates both its presence, its "somethingness" as a set, and also its absence, its nothingness, as a set with no elements. But by designating itself in this way – as the set of no elements, the set of nothing – the empty set also confers a somethingness to its contents (which are: nothing). These twists and turns in the logic allow a philosopher like Badiou to propose a philosophy based not on presence and somethingness (the tradition of Heidegger and Sartre), but on the void: "It is a question of names here – 'nothing' or 'void' – because being, designated by these names, is neither local nor global. The name I have chosen, the void, indicates precisely that nothing is presented, no term, and also that the designation of that nothing occurs 'emptily'..."[94]

Being and Time, Being and Nothingness, Being and Event. Imposing philosophical tomes of often-opaque, indecipherable language. But they also contain surprises within them – sometimes unbeknownst to the authors themselves. Though they differ in their approaches, Heidegger, Sartre, and Badiou all begin with that most basic of philosophical problems, "why is there something rather than nothing?" But they end up addressing a different problem: "what to do with nothing." And this on the two levels that Aristotle had long ago identified – the problem of "nothing" in the statement "there is *nothing*" and the problem of the statement "is" in "there *is* nothing."

The philosophical enterprise, which seemed, since antiquity, so concerned with the problem of being, has also revealed an equal, if more furtive concern with non-being, nothing, nothingness, and the void. Perhaps there is some truth to Sartre's words when he states that "nothingness haunts being."[95]

* * *

God is Nothing (Meister Eckhart). At this point, one could tread out a genealogy of nothing/nothingness in modern philosophy, noting how the insights of Heidegger, Sartre, and Badiou have found their way into contemporary discussions in speculative philosophy. But these contemporary discussions are in no way new. In fact, they often borrow from earlier, pre-modern philosophers. So, instead, we can step back and consider the question "why is there something rather than nothing?" in a different light.

Here we can examine the role of nothing/nothingness in the work of Meister Eckhart – philosopher, theologian, and heretic, who meditated at length on the philosophical problems that nothing/nothingness evoke. What is noteworthy in Eckhart's sermons is his use of the language of negation and nothingness, employed in a range of ways to describe God, creature, and an enigmatic "beyond" that Eckhart frequently calls the "Godhead" (*Gottheit*). In all cases Eckhart pushes for a non-anthropo-morphic, non-anthropocentric notion of nothing/nothingness that is, at the same time, not separate from the human being. While Eckhart's uses of the terms nothing, nothingness, and emptiness have garnered modern comparisons to Kierkegaard, Nietzsche, and Zen Buddhism, when placed in the context of mystical mediation, they taken on a specific set of meanings.[96]

Eckhart's sermons, in the theological tradition in which he was trained, isolate particular Biblical passages which Eckhart will then comment on in detail, developing a line of thought from a single phrase or even a single word. It is important to remain conscientious of this method when reading Eckhart. Our focus will be Eckhart's Sermon 19, where a passage from *Acts* 9:8 serves as the starting point for a commentary on the relation between the divine and "nothing." The passage in question is the following: "Paul rose from the ground and with open eyes saw nothing." A short but cryptic passage that appears straight-forward. The passage describes a mystical experience that entails three components: the mystical subject (Paul) in his relationship to himself; the act of "seeing" or of mediating between Paul and the divine; and that which Paul sees or which is mediated to Paul, which the passage enigmatically calls "nothing." In its form we have something completely quotidian, a human subject relating to an object through the mediation of sight, vision, and representation. But in its mystical context the passage deals not with the mediation of two like entities (e.g. both inscribed within time, both finite and bodily, both existing), but with two qualita-tively unlike entities. For this reason Eckhart focuses on the elusive object that is mediated, the "nothing" that is paradoxi-cally seen.

From this passage, Eckhart derives four meanings of the term "nothing" (*niht*):

> One is that when he rose up from the ground with open eyes
> he saw Nothing, and the Nothing was God; for when he saw
> God he calls that Nothing. The second: when he got up he saw
> nothing but God. The third: in all things he saw nothing but
> God. The fourth: when he saw God, he saw all things as
> nothing.[97]

These different senses of the term "nothing" are further elabo-
rated by Eckhart. He summarizes the first sense of the term
"nothing" in the following way: "He saw nothing, that is: God.
God is a nothing and God is a something. What is something is
also nothing."[98] This first sense is the most elaborate, in that it
deals with a philosophical notion of God as "Nothing," but a
nothing that is at the same time not simply negative or privative.
It is a notion of the divine in terms of a "nothing" that has little
to do with any ontological (or ontic) notion of nothing, in which
nothing is thought of in terms of the categories of being and non-
being, or being and becoming. Put simply, Eckhart's notion of
divine nothing is a non-philosophical notion that has "nothing"
to do with ontological categories of being and non-being, as well
as their modes or attributes, be they privative, subtractive, or
destructive. In this formulation, the divine is a nothing that is not
negative.

In fact, Eckhart's first formulation contains within it several
variations that elaborate this idea. In one variation Eckhart states:
"He saw nothing, that is: God." Here we have the assertion of a
divine unity that encompasses everything, including nothing,
and which itself is not reducible to a something or a nothing. The
fecundity of God is such that it encompasses that which is
without substance, that through which nothing flows forth. There
is no mystical experience in the sense of having an experience or
of containing something substantial that builds one up. Instead,

there is the self-abnegation or "releasement" of the subject, in which one finds a nothing "that is like finding God." This in turn leads to the necessity of thinking the divine as unrelated to the ontological categories of being and non-being – the God beyond Being, the Godhead beyond God. Hence in another variation Eckhart notes: "God is a nothing and God is a something." This is a recapitulation of the Dionysian assertion of the nameless God, the God without attributes or properties, the God to which no name is adequate. Eckhart, in other sermons, will frequently describe this God-beyond-Being as "the One."

And this leads to the limits of philosophical thinking itself, as it requires that the divine – the Nothing that is God, the God-beyond-Being – be thought of in terms of contradiction. Thus, in yet another variation, Eckhart says: "What is something is also nothing." Eckhart here assumes the inverse of this phrase – that nothing is also a something – and suggests that even this something (of nothing) is conditioned by a further nothing (or "Nothing"), that is the Godhead. Together, these variations all come under the Eckhartian assertion that "God is Nothing," comprising the first sense of the term "nothing."

Eckhart continues, summarizing the second sense of "nothing": "He saw God, in whom all creatures are nothing."[99] Whereas the first sense of "nothing" dealt with the divine in itself, here Eckhart describes a nothing that has to do with the relation between God and creatures. There is, certainly, a theological tradition of regarding creatures as "nothing" compared to God, in the sense that creaturely life is inscribed within temporality and finitude, life and death. This is the moral-theological notion of creaturely nothing. But Eckhart means more than this when describing creatures as nothing. Whereas in the first sense it is God that is nothing, here it is creatures that are nothing. But the nothing of creatures can be taken in several ways.

Here, Eckhart uses the language of representation and the

dichotomy between subject and object, image and thing. If the relation between any two creatures in the world relies upon the framework of subject and object, seer and seen, knower and known, then understanding creatures in God means understanding the relation between any two creatures as a mediated form of the relation between creature and God. One moves from the normative diagram of creaturely mediation – *creature A →creature B* – to the diagram of divine mediation – *creature A →[creature B] → God.* This is the pantheist – or really, panentheist – version of Eckhart. In so far as God is "in" all creatures, all creatures relate to God by relating to other creatures. This in turn opens onto the next stage, in which one effectively sees "through" creatures, effacing the creaturely mediation of God, as Eckhart says, one sees "nothing but God."

In the third sense of the term "nothing," Eckhart notes that "[s]eeing nothing, he saw God. The light that is God flows out and darkens every light... the Nothing was God."[100] Here Eckhart makes a transition from the relation between creatures and God, to the relation of creatures to God. Using the mystical motifs of darkness and light, Eckhart follows in the Dionysian-apophatic tradition by describing a superlative form of darkness or nothing that goes beyond the dichotomies of light/dark, something/nothing. Here one moves from optical sight to mystical vision, from a metaphysics of being to a non-metaphysics of nothing or "the One."

Finally, Eckhart summarizes the fourth and last sense of "nothing": "In seeing nothing, he saw the divine Nothing."[101] Here Eckhart suggests that the divine Nothing, being neither optical sight, nor representational thought, nor metaphysical substance, must ultimately remain both indifferent and indistinct. The "blindness" Eckhart references is both a turning away from the world (from regarding the world as substantial) and an emptying or "nothing-ing" of the self. Blindness is here an opacity, a total equivocity or non-relation between earthly and divine, creature and God. But this is not a nihilism, for this turning-away and self-emptying ultimately indicate the pervasiveness, the immanence, of the divine Nothing... in everything. Eckhart often returns to this condition of blind nothing, this gesture of "seeing nothing" with "eyes open."

* * *

Four Definitions of Nothing. In his commentary and exegesis on "nothing" Eckhart highlights one of the central problems in medieval philosophy – the nature of the relation between human and divine. In so far as the divine is conceived of in radically non-human terms (non-anthropomorphic, abstract, inaccessible, and "dark"), the divine is, in and of itself, not some thing among other things, not a being among other beings – the divine is, strictly, "nothing."

The dilemma, then, is how the human being, which is finite, actual, discrete, and bodied, how this human being can relate at all to the divine, when the latter has been characterized as nonrelatable. It would seem that either the divine would have to become more human-like, constraining itself into an anthropomorphic entity one can interface with (this is the theme of Christ as the God-man), or that the human being would have to divest itself of its boundaries and limitations in order to be adequate to the "nothing" of the divine (this is the theme of mystical *ec-stasis*, the self-abnegation of the mystic before God). It seems that the human-divine relationship is only possible at the cost of one of the terms negating itself (the human becoming more-than-human; the divine becomes less-than-divine), thereby rendering the relationship superfluous.

However, Eckhart, in several of his sermons, reminds us that the divine is not simply "out there," but also courses through the human being "in here." Strangely, this non-human divinity is within the human – it even constitutes the human, paradoxically forming its "ground." And here the dilemma is recapitulated: either the divine is immanently "in" the human, equal to the human (in which case there is no relation because everything is continuous), or the divine remains absolutely inaccessible in its "nothing," the human at best able to apprehend this inaccessibility as such.[102]

This dilemma, which reaches its peak in the question of mysticism, revolves around how "nothing" is defined, and this is the backdrop against which Eckhart parses his different definitions of "nothing":

First definition: the nothing of finite creatures. Creatures are "nothing" in the sense that they are created in time, and as time. Phenomenally, creatures exist in the world as flux and flow, as coming-to-be and passing-away (to borrow Aristotle's terms). This nothing is, as we've noted, the moral-theological notion, the devaluation of life and being, the "flight from creatures" advocated by theological orthodoxy. Nothing in this sense is *privative.*

Second definition: the nothing of creaturely being. Creatures are created in order to be (as Eckhart notes, "He created all things that they may be"). Thus there is a prior non-being that both precedes the creature and is its philosophical ground. Creatures are "nothing" in that they are founded on a primordial, pre-existent, non-being. Nothing in this sense is *subtractive.*

Third definition: the nothing of God. God is that which is outside of time, space, and modality. God is "nothing" in so far as God is not a being among other beings. But neither is God simply the supreme being or the most perfect being. God is, in this context, the Being of all beings, the superlative being whose particular, conditioning form of being bears little relation to the conditioned status of creaturely beings. Nothing in this sense is *superlative.*

Fourth definition: the nothing of the Godhead. Eckhart's own brand of apophaticism frequently puts him in a situation in which God alone is insufficient. There is, "beyond" God, the Godhead, to which no attributes, properties, or names can be given. Importantly, for Eckhart the metaphysics of being does not pertain to the Godhead. Eckhart often describes the Godhead as "the One." The Godhead, as the One, bears no relation to Being, or to Non-Being. In one sermon Eckhart asserts, "God is all, and is one."[103] Elsewhere he notes that the Godhead is "a non-God, a non-spirit, a non-person, a non-image; rather, He is a sheer pure limpid One, detached from all duality."[104] Here we can put forth a "heretical" reading of Eckhart. In this final sense of nothing, the nothing of finite creatures (first definition) is simply a pretext for the real identity or indistinction of the nothing of creaturely being (second definition) and the empty God (third definition). All of this is what is encompassed in the Eckhartian notion of nothing, in this final sense. The nothing of the now, the nothing of all that is. Nothing in this final sense is *nullifying*.

In traditional accounts of Christian mysticism, one is led to a dilemma, a fork in the road between two types of divine mediation: either that of there being no relation to the divine, or that of there being a relation to the divine, as nothing. With Eckhart, we see that this is a false dilemma – but one must abrogate some of the most basic principles of philosophical and theological thinking to reach this point. In our heretical reading of Eckhart, divine mediation has little to do with a negative that must be overcome by a positive. Instead, divine mediation is the collapse of negative and positive, subtractive and superlative, into the strange negative immanence, an immanence of nothing that Eckhart terms the Godhead. The Godhead: *nothing is everywhere*. Furthermore, for Eckhart this mediation leads not to despair, but is "joyful."

But Eckhart, too, runs into problems. For one, any careful reading of Eckhart must acknowledge that this talk about God as nothing, the immanent Godhead, and the arid, empty, unhuman desert is always doubled by an equal commitment to the Trinity, the *kenosis* or self-emptying of Christ, and a Person-oriented mysticism of Father, Son, and Human.[105] Put simply, the "philo-sophical" Eckhart is always correlated to the "theological" Eckhart. Both are, perhaps, brought into an uneasy relation, and it is this assemblage that constitutes the "mystical" Eckhart. Eckhart at once shores up the limits of the human while at the same time asserting a profound commitment to the human – but a human that is also a "letting-be," a human that is a "living without a why."

This tension is illustrated in Eckhart's different uses of the term "nothing." On the one hand, there is the nothing of creaturely life, the non-substantiality of what is ephemeral and temporary, the nothing of the all-too-human in its creaturely finitude. On the other hand, there is the nothing of the Godhead, the nothing that superlatively encompasses everything, including the very dichotomy of something/nothing, being/non-being. This is the nothing that is at once transcendent and immanent, the nothing that is at once the apophatic inaccessibility of the divine and the very ground of all that is, as it is. These resolve in a kind of dual-annihilation that is not simply negation. Bernard McGinn provides a summary:

> To say that creatures are nothing for Eckhart is to say that the existence they possess is a pure receiving. Poised between two forms of nothingness, the *nihil* by way of eminence that is God, and the *nihil* that marks the defect of creatures, Eckhart's mystical way will be an invitation to the soul to give up the nothingness of its created self in order to become the divine Nothing that is also all things.[106]

While we have outlined four usages of the term "nothing" in Eckhart, we could have also streamlined them into two, into a basic distinction between the nothing of creatures (of the human, of creaturely mediation) and the nothing of God (of the unhuman, of divine mediation). But even this division ultimately breaks down in Eckhart. The nothing of creatures immediately opens onto the nothing of the Godhead, collapsing the division into what Eckhart describes as the nothing of that which is, the nothing of "letting be." So, while our strong reading of Eckhart pushes for total indistinction and the paradoxical immanence of nothing, we must also note that, even in his most heretical moments, Eckhart still preserves a basic distinction between two types of nothing.

* * *

Logic of the Divine. As an exemplar of the tradition of negative theology, Eckhart frames mysticism as a form of mediation. But mediation in Eckhart is often unstable and in flux, as when the divine is characterized, in Neoplatonic terms, as fecund, generous, and flowing forth.[107] In these instances, mediation becomes so full, so complete, so characterized by generosity, that it paradoxically negates itself and all middle terms.

At other moments, mediation comes up against a limit, in which that which is mediated is rendered as opaque, obscure, and unintelligible. This "darkness" is not due to any privation or lack, but due to its alterity with respect to the human. The "divine darkness" is neither privative nor oppositional, but rather superlative, an indication of a limit to thought and to the human. The minimalist accessibility that remains can only be described in negative terms. Hence Eckhart's notions of the "silent desert" and the Godhead as a "nothing." This unhuman, apophatic limit is – at least in Eckhart – not simply another "out there," but fully immanent to all that is. One can only relate to it by not relating to it – indeed, by negating all forms of relationality. The nothing of the Godhead is, in Eckhart's terms, the "negation of negation," the indifference of the transcendent and immanent, a paradoxical immanence of "nothing." Hence mediation, while never ceasing to be mediation, becomes so "empty," so full of negation, that it is evacuated and becomes antimediation.

For Eckhart the condition of mysticism is the loss of self in the divine – or, more accurately, the emptying of the self or self-abnegation that parallels the emptiness or nothingness of the Godhead. Eckhart takes to the limit a motif commonly found in mystical texts – that of the mystical union as the dissolution of all differences, including the difference between self and God, the creaturely and the divine, the human and unhuman. With Eckhart, one divinizes the human, rather than humanizing the divine. For Eckhart, mysticism is a movement from the fullness of God to the nothing of the Godhead.

But we must remember that for Eckhart this mediation is really divine mediation, that is, the mediation not of two points within a single reality, but a mediation between two "realities," earthly and divine, natural and supernatural, the known and the unknown. But this comes with a few caveats: that the condition of the "other" reality being mediated must remain a limit (sometimes unintelligible, sometimes inaccessible, sometimes both), and that (as in Eckhart's version), the "other" reality being mediated is not "out there," not above or beyond, not another place to which one must travel or with which one must connect.

In Eckhart's sermons, there is a consistent – and paradoxical – assertion of the divine as inaccessible (in his motifs of the desert, the emptying of the self, the nothing of the Godhead). Eckhart maintains a minimal form of mediation, seen in his distinction between the two basic types of nothing (the nothing of creatures and the nothing of the Godhead). For Eckhart, divine mediation tends towards a logic of *both/and*: in the coincident nothing of Godhead and creatures, there is both the mediation of nothing, and the nothing that is mediation. All mediation is a pretext for the impossibility of mediation, one that, at times, becomes indissociable from pure immediacy.

In short, for Eckhart, *divine nothingness is that form of relation that questions relationality in and of itself.* In particular, divine mediation is unstable and wobbly, always tending towards either the impossibility of relation or pure relation, pure immediacy – or, occasionally, towards the very indistinction between them. Mysticism is that form of mediation that suggests to us that there is in fact no mediation as such, no steady-state or stable connection that we can, with any degree of confidence, call "mediation." In the parlance of modern communications theory, there are no fixed senders or receivers, no well-established channels, and no referential messages (or noise). The "mediation" of divine mediation is simply a way-station to either the fullness of mediation (and thus its negation as mediation) or the emptiness of mediation (and thus its affirmation as already realized). For mystical thinkers like Eckhart, mediation is always failing, flailing, and breaking down into the darkness of God or the equally incomprehensible luminosity of divine self-abnegation. One is confronted with the numinous, absolute opacity of the divine, or one is engulfed in the prodigious flux of divinity; one either confronts the black, viscous void of divine discontinuity, or one is set ablaze in the sparkling brilliancy of divine continuity. Complete difference or complete indifference – these are the poles of divine nothingness.

* * *

Metaphysical Correlation, Mystical Correlation. These aspects of divine mediation allow us to re-frame mysticism as a modern philosophical problematic. In the Western tradition, nearly every philosophical position, every philosophical "decision," every assertion of being, identity, or oneness, relies on a minimal relation between thought and world, self and other, subject and object. How exactly is the mediation of mysticism – divine mediation – different from the numerous examples of mediation one finds in philosophy? In other words, how is divine mediation different from metaphysical mediation? Both borrow the form of relationality that has now become the common parlance of modern communications theory (A connected to B via a medium X). Both also presume an apriori separation that subsequently requires some mediated correlation.

However, there is one possible way in which they differ. In traditional metaphysics we have the correlation between subject and object, within a given order of the real (thought and world, self and other, and so on). The "real" may be material or ideal, noumenal or phenomenal, visible or invisible, but however it is construed, it remains the condition of possibility for thought. Let us call this *metaphysical correlation*. Metaphysical correlation, in presuming a minimal mediation that makes thought possible, subscribes to a "principle of sufficient philosophy."[108]

And yet, with mysticism, we do not so much have mediation within a given real, as we have the correlation between different orders of the real, unilaterally posited as the relation between the real from the perspective of the human, and another real, that can only be termed the "unhuman." Let us call this *mystical correlation*. In theological terms, this relation may be between the natural and supernatural, the earthly and the divine, creature and Creator, and so on.

While both the mystical and the metaphysical borrow the form of mediation, what results in each is a different type of correlation between terms. In metaphysical correlation thought is always turned towards the world; thought is always "chasing" its correlate, on its trail, ferreting it out into the open – it is always a "thought of." In metaphysical correlation, thought is a *hunt*. In mystical correlation, by contrast, thought is always turned away from the world (or it is only turned towards the world in so far as the world *is* this other order of the real, the "out there" the same as the "in here"). In mystical correlation thought is always oriented towards something that is understood to be in excess of thought; thought is always in relation to its own negation. In mystical correlation, thought is a *sacrifice*.

Metaphysical correlation is always after a response that it has already posited before it begins the task of thinking. It is a self-fulfilling prophecy, a self-congratulatory gesture. It has caught its prey before the hunt has begun. By contrast, mystical correlation can never receive a response, precisely because it is after that which is simply without-thought (or non-thought). It can only succeed if it fails; there can only be affirmation if there is negation. If metaphysical correlation is agonistic, mystical correlation is ritualistic.

This is, granted, a bit cursory. But if mysticism is a relation between two orders of the real, two "reals," instead of a relation between two entities within a single real, then this means that the *intrinsic* relations of metaphysical correlation (self-world; human-human) are displaced or scaled up to the *extrinsic* relations of mystical correlation (earthly and divine; human-unhuman). This would remain the case even if the unhuman real is considered to be fully immanent to the human real.

Mystical correlation is a type of mediation that devolves around a limit. That limit is the unilateral "perspective" of the human real towards the unhuman real; a limit of the human towards something that it can only call the unhuman. This limit is neither relative nor absolute – or it is absolute only in its relativity (that is, absolute from the human perspective). This also means that the mystical correlation always fails. It is a loop that never closes, a spiral that never fully turns. It is a relation that can only be verified "from this side." It is a relation that is only verified in the blank, impersonal opacity of the "divine nothing," the wayless abyss, the "divine darkness."

From a contemporary perspective, what thinkers like Eckhart offer is a way of reconsidering a problem that is at once mystical and metaphysical – the problem of the anthropocentrism of thought. Eckhart presents us with a form of divine mediation as the form of relation between the human and the unhuman, a situation in which the fullest mediation and the impossibility of mediation become one in the same.

In relation to current philosophical trends, these two types of divine nothingness – as pure relation and pure opacity – are simply the premodern avatars of, respectively, a philosophy of continuity (the continentalist tendency towards immanence, vitalism, vibrancy, the phenomenology of affect) and a philosophy of discontinuity (the analytical tendency towards assemblages, objects, actants, and so on). But we can already see in thinkers like Eckhart a willingness to break down such distinctions, in his notion of the Godhead as the immanence of nothing, the divine as negative fecundity (a "negation of negation"), and the absolute opacity of "letting be" (of that which is what it is).

In so far as mysticism is concerned with the relation between two orders of the real (divine and earthly, supernatural and natural), it can be regarded as an instance of mediation. In some instances the divine is so in excess of the human that it can only be described as a total annihilation, a self-abnegation. Mediation is so in excess of itself that, paradoxically, mediation is annihilated, and becomes nothing. In other instances, the unhuman, divine element stands in such indifference and indistinction to the human, that only negative terms can be used to describe it – it is null and void, a gulf or abyss, a "nothingness" in which all that is mediated is the paradoxical impossibility of mediation itself. In one instance, we have a "full" nothingness, an immediacy or *immediation*; in the other instance, an "empty" nothingness, an *antimediation*. Together, these terms – mediation, immediation, and antimediation – describe the spectrum of mystical correlation, viewed primarily through an apophatic prism.

* * *

Death in Deep Space (The Kyoto School). There is a motif commonly found in horror and science fiction, one that historically derives from narratives of adventures at sea and tales of castaways. The motif is that of the sole human being, unmoored, set loose, and adrift in space. From the *Odyssey* and *Orlando Furioso* to the tales of nautical horror by Edgar Allan Poe, Jules Verne, and William Hope Hodgson, to contemporary science fiction and horror films, there is something terrifying about this sense of being cast adrift in deep space.

Science fiction and horror authors often depict "adrift in space" as being "lost in space," that is, as a by-product of intergalactic adventure narratives. One was only lost in space until the next adventure, the next battle, the next conquest. However, for earlier works – most notably Camille Flammarion's metaphysical science fiction tale *Lumen* (1873) – being adrift in space is less a by-way to yet another adventure, than a speculative opportunity in and of itself. Being adrift in space *is* the story itself, so much so that Poe could pen entire cosmic dialogues around the theme – such as "The Conversation of Eiros and Charmion" – without character, plot, or setting; abstract horror tales comprised entirely of metaphysical speculation.

Being adrift in space is not only a moment of horror, but also a moment of speculation. It is, first, a confrontation with the certitude of death. The lone body, drifting into deep space, will inevitably dissolve itself into that abyss, both literally and metaphysically. When one is lost at sea, there is at least the reliable dichotomy of surface/death or land/sea, to orient one's being lost. Similarly, when one is lost in space, one is simply moving from one planet to the next (using the reliable dichotomy of earth/sky), perhaps with the stars as one's guide. But the motif of being adrift in space lacks all these reference points. There is no ground, no horizon, no perspective – for that matter there is no depth of space itself, there is only blackness, an abyss that is at once flat and infinite. It is inaccurate to say that one is "in" empty space. It is even inaccurate to say that one is "in" emptiness.

This motif of being cast adrift is an allegory for a certain type of metaphysical crisis that goes by the name of "nothingness." As Pascal once noted, pondering the idea of infinity, "the eternal silence of these infinite spaces terrifies me." When a philosophy loses its ground – or when it discovers that the ground it had assumed is actually groundless – then philosophy is confronted with a few choices. It can accept this loss of ground as a fact, and then opt for either mysticism or science, poetry or facts. But there are also those philosophies that resist this move, and attempt to paradoxically subsist in the loss of ground. In the Western tradition thinkers such as Pascal, Kierkegaard, and Nietzsche are typically given as examples of this kind of thinking.

But there is also a whole tradition of non-Western thinking that engages with this question, specifically in the history of Japanese philosophy, where the intersection of Buddhist and European cultural influences produced one of the most fascinating philosophical approaches – that of the so-called Kyoto School.[109] At the center of many Kyoto School thinkers is the classical Buddhist concept of śūnyatā, frequently translated as "nothingness" or "emptiness." While Kyoto School philosophers were well-versed in Western philosophy, their development of this term differs as much from Heidegger and Sartre as it does from its original use in the Buddhist sutras. Contemporary philosopher Masao Abe summarizes this difference:

...in the West such positive principles as being, life, and the good have ontological priority over negative principles such as non-being, death, and evil. In this sense negative principles are always apprehended as something secondary. By contrast, in the East, especially in Taoism and Buddhism, negative principles are not secondary but co-equal to the positive principles and even may be said to be primary and central...

In short, the ultimate which is beyond the opposition between positive and negative is realized in the East in terms of negativity and in the West in terms of positivity.[110]

While comparisons like these are schematic, it does illustrate two things about the Kyoto School tradition: that many of the thinkers associated with it were as comfortable discussing Western metaphysics as they were the finer points of Zen Buddhism. Indeed, many of them were of a generation that allowed the free intermingling of a range of influences east or west. It is this that makes the Kyoto School thinkers uniquely situated to carry out studies in comparative philosophy.

At the center of the formation of the Kyoto School are three philosophers – Kitarō Nishida (1870-1945), Hajime Tanabe (1885-1962), and Keiji Nishitani (1900-90)[111] – each of whom brings with them some degree of training in Mahāyāna Buddhist philosophy generally, and Sōtō Zen in particular. The moniker of the "Kyoto School" seems to have been made quite early; scholars date it to a newspaper article from the 1930s describing Japan's new, modern thinkers. Then, as now, the term refers to a generation of philosophers who worked and taught at Kyoto Imperial University, and whose work brought together Western-European and Eastern-Buddhist ideas. Their influence also stretched outside of Japan – Nishida was a colleague and friend of D.T. Suzuki, who went on to popularize Zen in America, and both Tanabe and Nishitani studied and lectured outside of Japan.

One of the distinguishing aspects of the Kyoto School is their unique combination of Mahāyāna Buddhism and German Idealism. Nishida speaks frequently of "pure experience," Tanabe of "absolute mediation," and Nishitani of "absolute nothingness." The concept of the absolute haunts nearly all their works, whether they are discussing subjective experience or the physics of the material world. This development of a hybrid philosophical language was no accident. In the early 1920s,

Tanabe received a scholarship to study abroad, where he worked with the Kantian philosopher Alois Riehl, before turning to Husserlian phenomenology. Apparently, Tanabe was invited to Husserl's home to give a paper, where the latter hoped to make Tanabe a prophet of phenomenology to the East, a task to which Tanabe was not sympathetic. Tanabe eventually befriended a young Heidegger, who tutored Tanabe in German philosophy and introduced him to the works of Hegel, Fichte, and Schelling. Likewise, Nishitani grew up reading Dostoevsky, Schelling, Emerson, and above all Nietzsche, while also enjoying the novels of Natsume Sōseki. In the late 1930s Nishitani received a scholarship to study abroad with Henri Bergson. When news of the French vitalist's failing health reached Nishitani, he was offered an alternate choice: to go to the University of Freiburg to study with Heidegger. While the idea of having Heidegger as your second choice is amusing, Nishitani took the opportunity seriously. During this two-year period, Nishitani not only attended Heidegger's lectures on Nietzsche, but he wrote a thesis for Heidegger on Nietzsche and Meister Eckhart, perhaps one of the first sustained studies of its kind. While Japanese philosophy is much broader than the Kyoto School, the tradition continues to this day in the work of philosophers such as Masao Abe, Shin'ichi Hisamatsu, and Shizuteru Ueda.

* * *

Absolute Nothingness (Nishida). These cross-cultural elements make for a fascinating, if sometimes ambiguous example of what a post-national, global philosophy might look like. For the Kyoto School philosophers, this particular mix of influences is best exemplified by what is arguably their major contribution: the concept of nothingness. The term *śūnyatā*, conventionally translated into English as either "nothingness" or "emptiness," brings with it a whole host of meanings that are as much religious as philosophical. In the Mahāyāna Buddhist tradition, *śūnyatā* is the groundless ground of all things, the principle or essence that is not itself a principle or essence. For instance, one frequently-cited source for the Kyoto School thinkers is the 2nd-3rd century Indian logician Nagarjuna, whose major work *Mūlamadhyamaka-kārikā* (*The Fundamental Wisdom of the Middle Way*) defines *śūnyatā* through a rigorous logic of successive negations:

"Empty" should not be asserted.
"Nonempty" should not be asserted.
Neither both nor neither should be asserted.
They are only used nominally.[112]

This practice of successive negations are known as a tetralemma (or in Sanskrit as the *catuṣkoṭi*), and it is found throughout Nagarjuna's work, as well as in other texts in the Mahāyāna tradition, such as the *Heart Sutra*. The tetralemma involves, quite simply, four logical operations: an assertion *p*, its negation *not-p*, a double affirmation *both p and not-p*, and a double-negation *neither p nor not-p*. When applied to the difficult concept of *śūnyatā* the result is often dense, enigmatic phrases, such as:

If there were even a trifle nonempty,
Emptiness itself would be but a trifle.
But not even a trifle is nonempty.
How could emptiness be an entity?[113]

Without getting lost in the massive commentarial tradition on Nagarjuna, we might generalize *śūnyatā* and say that it is that which is prior to all duality of being and non-being, beyond all subsequent divisions of subject and object, and that which persists beyond or behind all that subsists as phenomena. But nothingness is also inherently self-negating; the thought of that which defies the very categories of thought, primary among them being Aristotle's famed principle of non-contradiction. Such a thought requires a deft philosophy able to handle the nuances of contradiction, as the Kyoto School thinkers would find not only in the work of Nāgārjuna, but also in Dōgen, the 13th century philosopher, teacher, and founder of Sōtō Zen.

But the Kyoto School philosophers were never content to simply add on Eastern ideas as a supplement to the Western canon, the former playing the role of the intuitive, poetic loosening of ideas, the latter establishing the rules and rigor of science. Instead, what we find is that each of the Kyoto School thinkers brings together disparate philosophical traditions in a way that ultimately questions philosophy *tout court*.

For Nishida, himself personally and professionally inspired by Zen, the challenge was discovering the common thread between Eastern and Western philosophy. Nishida's reference point here is Kant, and the impasse that Kantian critical philosophy poses between self and world, an impasse that Nishida is convinced can be re-thought. The path for doing this lies in Nishida's mixture of Zen and German Idealism, particularly the work of Fichte. The result is a strange Fichtean Buddhism:

> For some time now I had it in mind to try and explain all of reality in terms of pure experience... Along the way, I came to think that it is not that there is an individual that has the experience, but that there is an experience that has the individual, that experience is more basic than any distinction individuals bring to it. This made it possible to avoid solipsism, and by taking experience as something active, to harmonize it with transcendental philosophy after Fichte.[114]

The passage is from Nishida's best-known work, *An Inquiry into the Good*. Nishida's search for "a single, all-encompassing, acting absolute" led him first to question the categories of self and experience laid out by Kant and recapitulated by post-Kantian thinkers such as Fichte. Of course, the problem Nishida runs into quite early is the same one encountered by mystics when they speak of a mystical union with the divine. That problem is not just about psychologism, but about the tension between intuition and reflection, key terms in Kantian (and Bergsonian) philosophy: "As *intuition* it [the subject] needs to be aware of a flowing, continuous reality unbroken by subject or object, and as *reflection* it needs to step outside of the flow of reality to recognize it."[115]

Nishida's great insight was, perhaps, to be able to shift his direction: instead of establishing a continuum beyond subject and object from the inside-out, Nishida re-casts his method, moving from the outside-in. This shift is detected at the micro-level of Nishida's philosophical vocabulary, which in earlier texts favored phrases such as "pure experience" to talk about the anonymous, impersonal quality of experience. In *An Inquiry into the Good* and his later writings, Nishida reserves the phrase "absolute nothingness" to talk about this continuum underlying all divisions (not just of subject and object, but of being and non-being as well). Instead of attempting to reach the continuum as a subject would an object – a project destined to fail, since the Absolute that Nishida discusses is not, strictly speaking, an object – now Nishida opts for the language of negation, borrowed in part from his study in, and practice of, Zen Buddhism. In the practice of *zazen*, one does not so much "look at" nothingness, as one allows the nothingness that pervades all things, including the self, to emerge. In this way, it is through negation that Nishida attempts to move from psychology to ontology – a move echoed a century earlier by German Idealist philosophers.

Whether or not such a philosophy does escape the pitfalls of subjectivism or solipsism is up for debate; but in shifting his terms in this way and opting for a philosophy of negation,

Nishida's thought opens onto another problem, one different from that of subjectivism. That problem has to do with contradiction itself. The relation between contradiction and negation in philosophy has a long history, to be sure. But, if we are to follow Aristotle's and Kant's statements on the topic, it appears that even contradiction must observe certain rules, such that it can be inculcated within philosophy itself or domesticated within the strictures of logic. Contradiction must make a certain sense. The Kyoto School philosophers question even this. Thus, "to call reality itself *absolute nothingness*, then, is to say that all of reality is subject to the dialectic of being and not-being, that the identity of each thing is bound to an absolute contradictoriness."[116]

* * *

Towards Emptiness (Nishitani). In a sense, where Nishida leaves off, Nishitani begins. Also deeply influenced by Zen Buddhism, Nishitani was an attentive reader of Western thinkers such as Eckhart, Nietzsche, and Heidegger. More directly engaged with the social, cultural, and political issues of his time – though not without some controversy – Nishitani highlights the "problem of nihility" as it impacts modern Japanese culture.[117] It is from this basis that his own engagement with the concept of nothingness derives. Writing after the war, Nishitani notes that nihilism has come to mean something different in Japan. Whereas, as per Nietzsche's diagnosis, European nihilism emerges as the result of a crisis in religion and the ascendency of scientific rationality, in Japan the foundation has simply withered away, without a great announcement and without anything taking its place. It is, in a sense, the most perfected example of nihilism. While not nostalgic for this withering away of traditional religion, Nishitani notes that the manner in which religion has declined has given Japanese culture a different kind of nihilism. As Nishitani notes, "in the past, Buddhism and Confucian thought constituted such a basis, but they have already lost their power, leaving a total void and vacuum in our spiritual ground... The worst thing is that this emptiness is in no way an emptiness that has been won through struggle, nor a nihility that has been 'lived through.' Before we knew what was happening, the spiritual core had wasted away completely."[118]

At the same time, Nishitani notes that increasing techno-logical rationalization, along with the withering of traditional religions, has resulted in what he terms "the tendency towards the loss of the human." Reduced through science, manufactured through technology, and alienated in modern social relations, the human being, for Nishitani, finds itself everywhere in general but nowhere in particular. In addition, an increasing, global awareness of issues related to climate change and disasters, both natural and human-made, have rendered the idea of religion deeply problematic. Here an abyss opens up: "when this horizon does open up at the bottom on those engagements that keep life moving continually on and on, something seems to halt and linger before us. This something is the meaninglessness that lies in wait at the bottom of those very engagements that bring meaning to life."[119]

This abyss is what Nishitani terms "nihility." Nihility is the absence of any meaningful or necessary relationship between the human being and the world into which it is cast. This relationship of vacuity oversteps the scale of individual human beings or human collectivities; it is a vacuousness that oversteps the personal, resulting in what Nishitani terms an "impersonally personal" or "personally impersonal" relation. The human being, which had just prior taken the world for granted as its home, suddenly appears radically out of place, both in the world and in its very being:

While it continues to be the world in which we live and is inseparably bound up with our existence, it is a world in which we find ourselves unable to live as *man*, in which our *human* mode of being is edged out of the picture or even obliterated. We can neither take this world as it is nor leave it.[120]

With nihility the human being is stuck between two mutually untenable positions. It is clear that the world is not simply "our" world, the world made in our image, the world-for-us; but it is equally clear that we as human beings remain in the world, for better or worse. Is there, perhaps, a way in which we can make sense of the world – "so indifferent to our human mode of being as to rub it out" – but do so outside of our human meaning-making activities? This is where, for Nishitani, a philosophical question becomes an essentially religious one.

But traditional religions will not do, for they only ramify the problem by introducing indifferent, cruel, or law-enforcing gods. With nihility, the stakes are much higher than simply replacing one pantheon with another, one icon with another. Here Nishitani takes his cue from Nietzsche. Both identify a crisis that is as much a social, cultural, and political crisis as it is a philosophical one. Both agree that it will not do to simply set up a new idol (technology) to replace the old one (religion). And both agree that the way beyond nihilism is through nihilism. But, interestingly, whereas Nietzsche opts for an affirmative ontology of non-human will, force, and "quanta of power," Nishitani does nearly the opposite, and opts for a negative ontology filled with contradictions – a ground of emptiness, a religion without God, an ethics without selfhood. Nihility is as much as much an intuition of a subject as it is a statement about the world, "the point at which the nihility that lies hidden as a reality at the ground of the self and all things makes itself present as a reality to the self in such a way that self-existence, together with the being of all things, turns into a single doubt."[121] The very distinction between doubting subject and doubtful world dissolves, leaving only the "Great Doubt." As Nishitani notes, philosophy "needs to pass through nihility and shift to an entirely new field."[122]

What that new field is, is the subject of Nishitani's major work, *Religion and Nothingness*, at the core of which is a classical Buddhist term, *śūnyatā* (emptiness, nothingness). The problem, as Nishitani defines it, is not so much that there is nothing to believe in, or that our ways of making meaning about ourselves and the world are unreliable. Rather, the problem is the very structure of belief, the very structure of meaning-making. How, then, to proceed? Perhaps, the problem with being, is, in a way, being itself. Whereas Western philosophy concerns itself primarily with being, the philosophy that Nishitani points to concerns itself primarily with non-being or nothingness; whereas Western philosophy is centered around the question of ontology and the question of being ("why is there something rather than nothing?"), the philosophy that Nishitani is thinking of is a paradoxical ontology of non-being or nothingness ("why assume that there is anything at all?"). But this non-being or nothingness "cannot lie on a far side, beyond *this* world and *this* earthly life of ours, as something merely transcendent. It must lie on the near side, even more so than we ourselves and our own lives in the here and now are ordinarily supposed to be."[123] Nishitani is proposing something quite ambitious, a concept of non-being or nothingness that is neither opposed/contrasted to being (as in Heidegger), nor contained by it/nested within it (as in Sartre). As Nishitani notes, in "the Buddhist standpoint of *śūnyatā* ('emptiness'), this point comes to light still more clearly."[124]

The concept of *śūnyatā* has a long and complex history in Buddhist thought. One finds it, in various guises, in the discourses of the Buddha, in Mahāyāna canonical texts such as *The Heart Sutra* (*Prajñāpāramitā Hṛdaya*), and in the writings of Zen teachers such as Dōgen. Nishitani, along with his Kyoto School colleagues, takes up this term in a modern way, placing it alongside Western notions of nihilism (Nietzsche), nothing (Heidegger), and nothingness (Sartre). As we've noted, for

Nishitani the standpoint of *śūnyatā* takes as its starting point non-being rather than being, and in so doing already departs from the Western metaphysical tradition. This also means that, for Nishitani, *śūnyatā* cannot be regarded as equivalent to the terms non-being, nothing, or nothingness. It is not a non-being that is secondary to being (non-being is not derivative from or an error of being), and it is not a non-being that comes after being (non-being only existing by virtue of negating a prior being).

What then is *śūnyatā*? "Emptiness in the sense of *śūnyatā* is emptiness only when it empties itself even of the standpoint that represents it as some 'thing' that is emptiness."[125] In Nishitani's hands, *śūnyatā* enacts a double negation: a negation of being (and in particular, of substantialist notions of being that view it as prior to non-being), and then a negation of this negation, in effect negating the very relation between being/non-being, something/nothing, fullness/emptiness. Herein lies the difference between *śūnyatā* and terms such as nihility, nothing, nothingness. In nihility we have a "negative negativity" aimed at or in relation to being. "Its standpoint contains the self-contradiction that it can neither abide in existence nor abide being away from it."[126] By contrast, with *śūnyatā* there is a negation of the negation, "the standpoint at which absolute negation is at the same time... a Great Affirmation."[127] In *śūnyatā* one does not simply state that the self and all things are empty, since this would remain within the ambit of nihility (negating an affirmation). Instead of stating that the self is empty, in *śūnyatā* one states that emptiness is the self; instead of stating that all things are empty, in *śūnyatā* one states that emptiness is all things. The shift that Nishitani evokes here is subtle, but in his updating of the term *śūnyatā* he appears to be positing a kind of "empty" monism, a principle-of-every-thing that is, at the same time, nothing.

This is a tall order, to be sure. But the fact that this is so illustrates how ramified the problem is for Nishitani, not just in terms of philosophical habits, but in our everyday habits of thinking as well: "Ordinarily, of course, we occupy a standpoint shackled to being, from which being is viewed solely as being." When this becomes unstable, what Nishitani calls nihility breaks through. But then the temptation is to latch on to the inverse, to non-being as the sole reality and ground, and "this standpoint of nihility in turn becomes a standpoint shackled to nothingness."[128] This too needs to be negated, and this is where *śūnyatā* comes into play. We have negated the logic of *either/or* (either being or non-being is one true reality), and we have also negated the logic of *both/and* (non-being exists but within being). What remains but the logic of *neither/nor*? Strangely, *śūnyatā* emptied in this way, as neither this nor that, becomes "nothing" but what it is – it is such-and-such. "In this meaning, true emptiness is not to be posited as something outside of and other than 'being.' Rather, it is to be realized as something united to and self-identical with being."[129] Nishitani summarizes this point again later on in his book:

> The emptiness of *śūnyatā* is not an emptiness represented as some "thing" outside of being and other than being. It is not simply an "empty nothing," but rather an *absolute emptiness*, emptied even of these representations of emptiness. And for that reason, it is at bottom one with being, even as being is at bottom one with emptiness... And the things as they are in themselves... just what they are and in their *suchness*, are one with emptiness.[130]

At the same time, we have not simply been brought back into the fold of being, for *śūnyatā*, in its absolute negation, points to the indistinction between emptiness and fullness, non-being and being, something and nothing. This non-being cannot simply be privative or relative, else Nishitani has done nothing other than re-cast a tradition that runs from Plato to Kant. Neither can this nothingness be rooted in the subjective experience of ground-lessness, as one finds in Sartre. Instead, *śūnyatā* has to be understood as "the nullification of the self by the nullification of the ground it has to stand on." This in turn leads to a further stage in which "that nihility is itself nullified... in the awareness that the world of being that rests on the nihility of the self and all things is only a relative manifestation of nothingness as it is encountered *in* reality."[131] Put simply, *śūnyatā* is non-being that is indistinguishable from being.

As with his colleagues Nishida and Tanabe, with Nishitani we find a preoccupation with a subtractive monism, a sense that "beneath that world, all around it, there is an encompassing absolute nothingness that *is* reality. Nihility is emptied out, as it were, into an absolute emptiness, or what Buddhism calls *śūnyatā*."[132] This is also the case in later generations of Kyoto School thinkers, many of whom adopt different approaches and methodologies, but still retain the insights of Nishitani's work on *śūnyatā*. For instance, Masao Abe, borrowing from analytical philosophy as well as from Buddhist sources, reiterates the contradiction in the concept of *śūnyatā*: "Emptiness as *śūnyatā* transcends and embraces both emptiness and fullness. It is really formless in the sense that it is liberated from both 'form' and 'formlessness.'" Pulling almost verbatim from the *Heart Sutra*, Abe continues, stating that "in *śūnyatā*, Emptiness as it is is Fullness and Fullness as it is is Emptiness; formlessness as it is is form and form as it is is formless... true Emptiness is wondrous Being."[133]

Similarly, in a comparison of "nothingness" in Meister Eckhart and Zen Buddhism, Shizuteru Ueda notes how the concept of *śūnyatā* runs against the "substance-thinking" of Western philosophy (inclusive of philosophies of process, change, or becoming). As he notes:

Absolute nothingness is concerned with the coincidence of ceaseless negation and straightforward affirmation, such that the coincidence as such is neither negation nor affirmation...

Put in philosophical terms, it [śūnyatā] refers to the negation of negation, which entails a movement in two directions at the same time: (1) the negation of negation in the sense of a further denial of negation that does not come back around to affirmation but opens up into an endlessly open nothingness; and (2) the negation of negation in the sense of a return to affirmation without any trace of mediation.[134]

The lengths to which Nishitani was willing to go in his development of the concept of nothingness inevitably led him to think about religion. However, while all the Kyoto School thinkers drew in different ways on Buddhism, they were in disagreement about the relation between philosophy and religion. In a way, they replay the debates of medieval Christian philosophers concerning the proper relation between faith and reason. In Nishida's more poetic works, philosophy tends to turn into religion, while at other times it is philosophy's function to explicate the truths revealed in religion. For Tanabe, who remains more committed to the scientific rigor of philosophy, religion and philosophy are analogous but separate endeavors. However even Tanabe implies that if the "absolute insolence" and freedom of philosophical thought is pursued to its extreme, it enters into a shared space with religion. Nishitani takes yet another position: "nothingness is deepened to the point that it can assault the very throne of God. The nihility that has untied itself from any and all support wrestles with God for authority and succeeds in offering itself as the absolute groundless ground."[135]

One senses that, for Nishitani, there is a horizon of thought shared by religion and philosophy, though they may each come to that horizon from different places. There is, perhaps, another history of philosophy to be written, one that would begin not from an ontology of being or becoming, but from a negative ontology – or really, a dark meontology (from the negative prefix

me-) for which contradiction is, paradoxically, not only fundamental but also necessary. On this point Nishida is perhaps the
clearest: "I think that we can distinguish the west to have
considered being as the ground of reality, the east to have taken
nothingness as its ground."[136]

4

Prayers for Negation

What Should Not Be. In the depths of labyrinthine caves, embedded in gigantic rocks, buried in the hottest geothermal vents, and in the cold stellar dust of space, life is stealthily creeping. In environments in which it was previously assumed that life could not exist, scientists have discovered a whole range of life forms that not only survive, but actually flourish under conditions of extreme heat, cold, acidity, pressure, radioactivity, and darkness. Their very existence suggests to scientists scenarios that for we human beings can only ever be speculative: the emergence or the extinction of life on the Earth, the adaptation of life forms to extreme environmental and climate changes, the existence of life on other planets or in outer space.

Dubbed "extremophiles," such organisms have been recently discovered by scientists working in a range of fields, from micro-biology and oceanography to lesser-known fields such as abiogenesis and astrobiology. Their discoveries have garnered attention both within and outside the scientific community, primarily because in many cases their findings end up questioning the basic premises of the life sciences, let alone our everyday notions of what can or cannot possibly be alive.[137] A recent scientific report, *Investigating Life in Extreme Conditions*, provides the decidedly non-human setting for understanding extremophiles:

> ...that part of the Earth's biosphere permanently inhabited by human beings is rather small and most of the planet, its deep core or mantle, will clearly never see a living organism. In between these two zones (inhabited and uninhabited), a variety of environments exist where human beings cannot

live permanently, or physically access, although other forms of life exist within them.[138]

The report goes on to define an extreme environment as "a given environment, where one or more parameters show values permanently close to the lower or upper limits known for life."[139] Extremophiles are united by the fact that they constitute novel forms of life that exist in conditions that would be unfavorable if not fatal to most life forms. In some cases scientists have discovered microbes that appear to live without sunlight or even oxygen: a group of bacteria called autolithotropes, for example, live deep within rock formations and derive all their nutrients entirely from granite, while the bacterium *Desulfotomaculum* thrives in the darkness of radioactive rocks.[140]

As living beings whose existence questions life, extremophiles pose interesting problems for philosophy – they serve as philosophical motifs, or philosophemes, that raise again the enigmatic question, "what is life?" Extremophiles are, quite simply, forms of life living in conditions antagonistic to life. Microbes existing in the conditions of the absence of light or oxygen – indeed, feeding off of the absence of light or oxygen – are an anomaly for biological science. And their anomalous existence as scientific entities invites us to raise not only philosophical questions, but, more specifically, questions pertaining to logic as well.

Extremophiles are contradictions. They are alive, but should not be alive. That is, they are alive according to our existing criteria of "life" and yet, according to those same criteria, they are not alive – or rather, they should not be alive. In classical Aristotelian logic, extremophiles transgress the basic laws of philosophical logic. Aristotle's famous Law of Non-Contradiction (LNC) states that for any entity p, the statements "p is true" and "p is false" cannot both be the case. And yet, here we have the *Desulfotomaculum* bacteria, which is both alive and not alive, according to the same set of scientific presuppositions concerning "life." Similarly, Aristotelian logic states the equally-famous Law of the Excluded Middle (LEM), which states that p is either true or false, one or the other, but not both at the same time. And yet the *Desulfotomaculum*, something which, according to current scientific criteria, shouldn't be alive, is alive, and even thriving.

Biological science, in so far as it is rooted in systematic description and classification, relies on its own principle of sufficient reason, namely that life and logic bear some basic relation to each other – in other words, the principle that all that can be identified and known as life is ordered or organized in such a way that it can live. The extremophiles are, in a way, examples of living contradictions, a living instance of the inverse relationship between logic and life.

Though Aristotelian logic has arguably been superseded by modern developments in logic, these so-called laws of thought still form the foundation for any general notion of philosophical rigor; they are the basis for the very possibility of anything like philosophy taking place at all. Without them, philosophy literally loses its ground, and collapses inward. And at the center of the example of extremophiles is not just the relation between logic and life, but, more specifically, the role that *negation* plays in this relationship.

But negation is a strange entity, or, we should say, a non-entity. It is often assumed to have a reactive, derivative function, which first presumes the existence of a positivity, which can then be negated. This is as much the case in examples of classical negation as it is in contemporary philosophy. For instance, Benjamin Noys suggests that contemporary theory, as diverse as it is, betrays a common commitment to "affirmationist" thinking, in which negation is always subsumed within affirmation. Such affirmationism affirms "the creation of unashamedly metaphysical ontologies, the inventive potential of the subject, the necessity for the production of novelty, and a concomitant suspicion of the negative and negativity."[141] The result is that negation comes to be automatically viewed as a failed or reactive affirmation – as self-impressed deconstruction, as a dialectical "paleo-Hegelianism," or simply as the "endorsement of nihilistic destruction."[142]

Furthermore, it is not clear if negation is an actual entity in the world, or simply a statement about entities, a functional operation. According to the conventional, Aristotelian understanding, affirmations are statements about the world or entities in the world ("p exists"), whereas negations are statements about statements ("p does not exist" or $\neg p$ is merely the negation of the statement "p exists"). This is because the statement "p does not exist" does not itself point to anything that exists, except the enigma of "not existing." The very thing that the laws of thought are supposed to prevent seems unavoidable when dealing with negation.

And yet, major philosophers of logic, from Aristotle and Kant down to Frege, Russell, and contemporary "dialetheists" all accept the central role not just of negation, but of contradiction, in any study of philosophical logic.[143] Though we may subsume negation within the ambit of philosophy, giving us a philosophy of negation, we must also ask at what point does negation *exceed* philosophy, perhaps undermining it and giving us a negation of philosophy? For every form of negation, then, it would seem that a "non-philosophy" would be required to comprehend it in all its complexity. But such a negation of philosophy can be taken in a number of ways, either as evoking a "pre-philosophical" mode prior to the divisions of subject and object, self and world, or as promising a "post-philosophical" mode in which such divisions are at last overcome in a grand synthesis. But these are the philosophical fantasies engendered by negation and its ambivalent threat. "Each philosophy," notes François Laruelle, "defines then a non-philosophical margin that it tolerates, circumscribes, reappropriates, or which it uses in order to expropriate itself: as beyond or other to philosophical mastery."[144]

This itself leads to a conundrum, since the laws of thought safeguard the coherence of philosophical claims, and yet any study of philosophy must necessarily acknowledge the centrality of negation and contradiction in a philosophical inquiry. Wittgenstein encapsulates this conundrum: "...it is important that the signs p' and $'\neg p'$ can say the same thing. For it shows that nothing in reality corresponds to the sign $'\neg'$."[145] In short, the laws of thought exclude those things that are constitutive of the laws of thought. And yet, what negation itself indexes is, strictly speaking, nothing – which, logically speaking, still exists (as "nothing"). Wittgenstein again: "The propositions $'p'$ and $'\neg p'$ have opposite sense, but there corresponds to them one and the same reality."[146]

Hence the relation of logic and life is of particular interest, for "life" is, arguably, *the* principle of affirmation. It is generative, proliferating, productive and reproductive, and when negation is considered – as organismic death or decay – it is recuperated into the affirmative model of life (e.g. cycles of life, evolutionary adaptation, participation in a larger ecosystem). For every negative, a positive, and for every negation an opposing affirmative term that ultimately subsumes it within the larger positivity of living beings. The idea that life would be constituted by and through negation would seem to be an anomaly, if not a logical impossibility. What if extremophiles are in fact the norm, and not the exception? A contradiction seems to haunt the concept of life.

* * *

On Absolute Life. However, we need not delve into the deepest caves or the most obscure corners of logic to discover contradiction at the heart of life. It is a core part of philosophical reflection on life, from Aristotle to Kant to contemporary biophilosophy. For instance, Aristotle's enigmatic *De Anima*, rendered more enigmatic by generations of commentary and translation, is perhaps the first systematic ontology of life that hinges on contradiction – namely, one between a general life-principle or life-force (*psukhē*) and the manifold instances of the living, so exhaustively catalogued in works such as *Historia Animalium*. The former (Life) is never present in itself, only manifest in the diverse concretions of the latter (the living); the latter serve as the only conceptual guarantee of the former. But it is Kant's treatment of the teleology or purposiveness of life (*zweckmäßigkeit*) that not only revives Aristotle's problematic, but adds another dimension to it – any instance of life is always split between its purposiveness in itself and its purposiveness for us, the beings who think life. In the Kantian paradigm, the possibility of knowing the former is always compromised by the presumptions of the latter.

On the one hand life is phenomenal since we as subjects are also living subjects. Life is amenable to the manifold of sensation, is given as an object of the understanding, and results in a synthetic knowledge of the nature of life. Life is an object for a subject. On the other hand, the Aristotelian problem – what is the life-in-itself that is common to all instances of the living? – returns again in Kant's critical philosophy. Life-in-itself is neither the knowledge nor the experience of the living (be it biological classification or the subjective phenomenon of living), and life-in-itself is also not the living being considered as such (e.g. the object given to science as an object of observation).

In short, it would seem that the life common to all living beings is ultimately enigmatic and inaccessible to thought, since any given instance of the living (as subject or object) is not life-in-itself, but only one manifestation of life. It seems there is some residual zone of inaccessibility that at once guarantees that there is a life-in-itself for all instances of the living, while also remaining, in itself, utterly obscure.[147] It is precisely as living subjects, with life given as objects for us as subjects, that we are cut off from, and yet enmeshed within, life in itself.

Schopenhauer once noted that Kant's greatest philosophic contribution was the division between phenomena and noumena, the world as it appears to us, and the enigmatic and inaccessible world in itself. Whereas for Kant this division served a critical or regulatory function, providing philosophy with ground to stand on, for Idealism this division is an impasse to be overcome – by and through philosophy itself.

We know that, for the generation immediately following on the coattails of Kant, the important task was to identify this split as the key impasse in Kantianism, and to provide ways of overcoming that impasse.[148] This is a significant project, because for Kant, the critical philosophy was not, of course, a problem, but rather a solution to a whole host of metaphysical quandaries that pitted empiricists against rationalists, materialists against idealists, and so on. In a sense, German Idealism's first and most important gesture is to restate Kantianism as a problem to be overcome. The concept of the Absolute, and the various avatars of the Absolute proposed by Fichte, Schelling, and Hegel (Spirit, the Infinite, the World-Soul), have to be understood as the outcome of this initial gesture.

But this split between phenomena and noumena can only be overcome if it is in some way collapsed – or rendered continuous. Since we as thinking subjects cannot have access to noumena, we must begin from phenomena, and in particular the phenomena of thought. Hence thought must not be taken as split from the world in itself, but as somehow continuous with it. But this itself is a difficult thought, precisely because thought is presumed to be specific to living, rational, human subjects – thought is internalized, rendered proprietary, owned and instrumentalized. Kant's split implicitly relies on an internalist model of thought, one that begins and ends with the philosophical decision of anthropocentrism.

The key move that Idealism makes is to externalize thought, to render it ontologically prior to the individual thinking subject that thinks it. Only if thought is understood to be ontologically prior to the human, only if thought is ontologically exterior to the human, can it then become that continuum between the "for us" and the "in itself," phenomena and noumena. The Idealist operation is, in a sense, to subtract the noumenal from the Kantian split, leaving only a continuum that stretches without demarcations between the world-for-us and the world-in-itself.

In place of the phenomena-noumena split, then, one has a new totality, which raises thought above its Kantian, anthropocentric bias, and establishes it as that which enables the very split between phenomena and noumena, as well as the split within phenomena between thought and world, and subject and object. Thought is raised to the Absolute, and, in this continuum, the thought of a subject and the world in itself are both manifestations of a single Absolute. If this is the case, then Kant's epistemological framework is not just a reflection or representation of the world, but is itself a manifestation of the Absolute. What results is a new kind of philosophical drama, a drama of the Real and the Rational (and their co-mingling), or, in Schelling's terms, a drama of Nature as the manifestation of the Absolute.

This continuum is neither a transcendent, static category of Being, nor is it simply an affirmation of an unbounded, immanent multiplicity of beings; it attempts to play the role of both an inaccessible noumena "outside" us, and a manifest field of phenomena that constitutes us from within. It is for this reason that Idealism turns to the concept of life-in-itself. For post-Kantian Idealism, the concept of life-in-itself establishes a continuum between phenomena and noumena, but without reducing itself to either biology or theology. For the early Hegel, the Absolute is inherently dynamic, "the life of the Absolute," moving, flowing, and becoming through the structured phases of the dialectic, with the living organism its exemplar.[149] For Schelling, with his long-standing interest in natural philosophy, it is in and through the process and expressive forces of nature that the Absolute manifests itself – thus Nature is "manifest Spirit" and Spirit is "invisible Nature."[150] Even Fichte, otherwise a logician, attempts to account for the movement between the I and not-I, the Ego and non-Ego, by resorting to the vitalist language of life itself, commenting on the "Absolute Life" through which the I/Ego spontaneously manifests itself.[151]

In its attempts to overcome the Kantian problematic, Idealist thinkers exhibit a conceptual shift from a static to a dynamic ontology, or from being to becoming; they also effect a shift from a transcendent to an immanent concept of life, in which the framework of source/manifestation supersedes that of essence/existence. They turn their attention to conceptual models borrowed from natural philosophy and the philosophy of the organism, which has the broad impact of shifting the philosophy of life from a mechanist framework to a vitalist one.

Within Idealism "life" becomes an ontological problematic, and in the process becomes a metonym for the Absolute, resulting in what we can simply call, following Fichte, *Absolute Life*. This Absolute Life is monistic; it is a metaphysical totality that underlies all reality, but that is not separate from it. It is a totality that exists beyond any part-whole relation, but that is also only ever manifest in the particular. This Absolute Life is also immanence; it is an infinite process of becoming, flux, and flow, an infinite manifestation in finite Nature, an infinite expression of the living in an organic whole called Life. Finally, Absolute Life is paradoxical. It harbors a conceptual duplicity in which Absolute Life is at once omni-present and omni-absent, accessible and inaccessible to the senses, thinkable and an outer limit for thought. Absolute Life, while not a pure thing-in-itself, is only ever manifest in Nature (and thus indirectly knowable). At its core, Absolute Life must necessarily have the conceptual structure of negative theology.

* * *

The Ontology of Generosity. If we had to give a name to this kind of thinking, in which life itself is ontologized beyond its regional discourses (e.g. natural philosophy, biology, zoology), and comes to serve as a metonym for the Absolute, we could call it the ontology of generosity. The ontology of generosity states, first, that the precondition of the intelligibility of life lies in its innate propensity for continually asserting itself in the living. This propensity applies as much to the upscale processes of growth and development as it does to the downscale processes of decay and decomposition; indeed, as Schelling often notes, life is never more strongly asserted than in the process of decay. Life, then, is generous, not simply because it always gives itself forth, but because it always asserts and affirms itself, even as it withdraws, withers, and returns to its inorganic foundations – where another life then continues. In the ontology of generosity, life is not simply present, but *overpresent*.

In post-Kantian Idealism, the ontology of generosity begins from these premises: the overpresence of life-in-itself, and the split between Life (as superlative to the living) and the living (as always in excess of Life). However, the generosity of life does not flow forth in a single, homogeneous manner. In a number of the *Naturphilosophie* works of Schelling and Hegel, one can detect several variations to the generosity of Life. Each variation is defined by a basic philosophical question that serves as its principle of sufficient reason. There is, first, *Life as genesis* (also generation; production). Life is generous because it is defined by an ontology of becoming, process, and genesis. Here the question is "why is there something new?"[152] This mode is especially evident in Schelling's work in natural philosophy, where a "speculative physics" aims to account for the flux and flows of the Absolute in and as Nature. Life is ontologically prior to the living, but Life is also only ever explained in the living. When Schelling discusses the "potencies" (*Potenz*) of Nature – forces of attraction and repulsion, dynamics of electricity and magnetism, organismic physiology – he is evoking the generosity of Life in terms of its geneses.

In addition to this, there is a second mode, in which *Life is givenness* (also gift, donation). In this case, Life is generous because it is defined by its being given, its giving forth, its being already-there, its affirmation prior to all being. Here the central question is "why is there already something?" The idea of givenness is the spectral backdrop of the concept of Absolute Life. It enables the thought of Life to pass beyond the regional philosophies of nature and obtain a superlative ontological status. That this or that particular instance of the living is given is no great statement; it only points to the need for a concept of Life to account for all possible instances of the living. That Life (as opposed to the living) is given is another issue altogether; it means that the Absolute is not only an intelligible totality, but that it is such within an ongoing process, an ordered flux and flow that is consonant with Absolute Life. In Hegel's epic schema, Spirit can only realize itself through its successive stages (Idea, Nature, Spirit) by virtue of this "life of the Absolute." Givenness is the necessary precondition for thinking Absolute Life.

The problem is that while Idealism provides a solution to the Kantian problematic, that solution often ends up being compromised by the Kantian framework itself. There is, to begin with, the problem of genesis – generosity demands genesis, if only as its minimal condition. Within the ontology of generosity, one must still posit a source of life, even if this source is self-caused or self-generating, even if genesis remains immanent to itself. There is also the rather nagging problem of teleology. The positing of a life-source necessitates the positing of an end or purpose to organization, in order to qualify and to justify the organization inherent in life – order demands an end. This is true even if the end one posits is the process of becoming itself, without end. The positing of a source and end dovetail into the need to accept a minimally causal distinction between source and end, and this remains the case even if one asserts an immanent relation between source and end, in which source and end persist in a kind of tautology.

The result is that the ontology of generosity inherited from German Idealism looks to be a compromised Kantianism, at once inculcated within the requirements of the Kantian framework and, at the same time, claiming to have absolved Kantianism of its own antinomies. In terms of the concept of life, the ontology of generosity must make do with a source that is self-caused, a process that is its own end, and an immanent distinction between essence and existence. The Idealist resolution of Absolute Life comes to resemble an ouroboros – a split that is rendered continuous, only to have the split swallow its own tail, and be recapitulated at a higher level.

With post-Kantian Idealism, then, we see the concept of life raised up, as it were, beyond the regional discourses of natural philosophy, such that it can serve as a continuum bridging the Kantian gulf between phenomena and noumena. But this requires that one think not just of this or that living being, but Absolute Life – that which is not reducible to, and yet not separate from, the fluxes and flows of life as we know it. Idealism's ambition is to put forth a concept of Absolute Life via an ontology of generosity, in which Life is conditioned affirmatively and positively by its overpresence. Absolute Life is thus overpresent in several ways – as genesis or as givenness. Note also that these two paths – genesis and givenness – also form the two major channels through which flow contemporary biophilosophies, with Life-as-genesis constituting the vitalist ontologies of Henri Bergson, Alfred North Whitehead, and Gilles Deleuze, and Life-as-givenness constituting the phenomenological approaches of thinkers such as Edmund Husserl, Jean-Luc Marion, and Michel Henry.[153]

* * *

On Ascensionism. How does the ontology of generosity attempt to resolve the problem posed by Kant, the irrevocable split between Life and the living? Put simply, the Idealist philosophies of Fichte, Hegel, and Schelling attempt to expand and to raise up the concept of life, to the point that "life" becomes identical with nature, the world, and even with being itself. In other words, life for these thinkers is not reducible to its biological, anthropological, or zoological definitions. Life is also not exclusive to the subjective, human experience of being alive (that is, to a life experience). In post-Kantian philosophy, the concept of life oscillates between these regional concepts (life science, life experience) and a more fundamental concept encapsulated in the phrase "Absolute Life." Life is elevated and raised up, beyond the human and beyond nature, even beyond the divine. We can call this kind of thinking *ascensionism*, as it denotes the process by which the concept of life is raised up to the status of a metaphysical principle. Ascensionist thinking has two forms, both of which we can still see today.

The first form of ascensionism states that *the world is alive*. By this is meant the process by which the concrete is raised up to the abstract. Thus the concrete notion of life as defined within natural philosophy or life science, is raised up and expanded so as to describe the world itself. One begins with the individuated living organism, and scales it up to the planetary level. In the history of philosophy, animism, panpsychism, and certain strands of phenomenology are examples of this first form of ascensionism. In science, a well-known example might be the Gaia hypothesis, as well as certain aspects of deep ecology.

The second form of ascensionism states that *life is the world*. This is the near inverse of the first form. Here we see the raising up of life as the privileged manifestation of a metaphysical principle, such as time and temporality, form and causality, or the concepts of becoming, process, and immanence. In philosophy, vitalism, mechanism, and pantheism might be examples of this second form of ascensionism. In science, one might cite certain aspects of biocomplexity and systems biology as examples.

Both forms of ascensionism are readily present in post-Kantian philosophy. Indeed, they imply one another. For instance, Hegel's comments on the organicist "life of the Absolute" in the *Phenomenology of Spirit* are linked to his study of living organisms in the *Philosophy of Nature*. Kant himself engages in ascensionist thinking when, for instance, he states that the principle of order in the world must be sought in the "analogue of Life" – in which life serves as the model for the ordered, purposive character of the world as a whole.

The ontology of generosity, expressed in ascensionist thinking, is not without its own limitations. Primary among these is the investment in an affirmative ontology with regard to the concept of life (whether it be in terms of genesis or givenness). So much is this a veritable apriori of the ontology of generosity, that in some cases it tends to become a *moral* principle as well – life is good precisely because it is fecund, generous, bountiful, and gives itself forth. We must have faith in life, go with the flow, and so on. And we as human beings become dubiously romanticized within this bountiful flux and flow, resulting in a lyrical and therapeutic anthropomorphism of the Absolute. In this heady mix of hippie-affectivism and chaos theory, the human expands to such an extent that it eclipses the world itself, absorbing the nonhuman into its embrace, able to know all and to be all.

Thus, while German Idealism provides a solution to the Kantian problematic, that solution often ends up being compromised by the Kantian framework itself. There is, for instance, the problem of causality. Within the ontology of generosity, one must still posit a source of life, even if this source is self-caused or self-generating. There is also the problem of teleology. This positing of a life-source necessitates the positing of an end or purpose, in order to qualify and to justify the organization inherent in life – order demands an end. This is true even if the end one posits is the process of process itself, the becoming of becoming itself. The positing of a source and end dovetail into the need to accept a distinction between source and end, and this is still the case even if one asserts an immanent relation between source and end.

The result is that the ontology of generosity inherited from German Idealism looks to be a compromised Kantianism. In relation to the concept of life, the ontology of generosity must make do with a source that is self-caused, a process that is its own end, and an immanent distinction between essence and existence. The question here is whether there are any alternatives to the ontology of generosity and its ascensionist thinking, a form of thinking in which "life" is always the "life-for-us" as human beings. But is it possible to have done with the concept of life? Is it possible to have something like a negative ontology of life, an ontology of life as, simply, nothing?

* * *

Schopenhauer's Antagonisms. At this point, the question is whether there is a post-Kantian response that does not adopt the ontology of generosity; and this is linked to a related question, whether there is a post-Kantian response that refuses refuge in a renewed concept of Being. When life is thought as life-in-itself, we seem to be driven to a fork in the road: either the framework of Being/beings or the framework of Being/becoming. There is, possibly, another approach, one that would think life-in-itself *meontologically*, as "nothing," though it too has its own limitations. The best exemplar of this approach is found in the work of Arthur Schopenhauer.

Schopenhauer's sentiments regarding German Idealist thinkers is well known. He despised them.[154] Certain passages in

The World as Will and Representation (hereafter *WWR*) betray a profound personal distaste towards Fichte, Schelling, and above all Hegel, for whom Schopenhauer reserves his most vitriolic phrases:

> ...the greatest disadvantage of Kant's occasionally obscure exposition is that... what was senseless and without meaning at once took refuge in obscure exposition and language. Fichte was the first to grasp and make vigorous use of this privilege; Schelling at least equaled him in this, and a host of hungry scribblers without intellect or honesty soon surpassed them both. But the greatest effrontery in serving up sheer nonsense, in scribbling together senseless and maddening webs of words, such as had previously been heard only in madhouses, finally appeared in Hegel. It became the instrument of the most ponderous and general mystification that had ever existed, with a result that will seem incredible to posterity, and be a lasting monument of German stupidity.[155]

Metaphysical rants like these occur throughout Schopenhauer's writings, and there is an argument to be made for a certain charm behind Schopenhauer's curmudgeonly dismissals. Indeed, for many readers "obscure exposition" and "ponderous mystification" have come to define philosophy itself. Certainly Schopenhauer himself appears to be no stranger to the crime of obscurity, as demonstrated by his frequent uses of terms like *qualitas occulta* and *principum individuationis*.

Despite this, there is also a sense of clearing the air in Schopenhauer's writings, and no doubt "untimely" followers of Schopenhauer such as Nietzsche found inspiration in this tone. Not so fast, quips Schopenhauer, we have not even begun to address the problems put forth by Kant's antinomies. In the opening of *WWR* Schopenhauer's first step is to brush aside the entirety of post-Kantian dogmatism and return to Kant's problematic – the split between phenomena and noumena. As he notes, "Kant's principal merit is that he distinguished the phenomenon from the thing-in-itself, declared this whole visible world to be phenomenon, and therefore denied to its laws all validity beyond the phenomenon." This is, notes Schopenhauer, an acceptable constraint to our metaphysical thinking. But why stop there? As Schopenhauer notes, it is "remarkable that he [Kant] did not trace that merely relative existence of the phenomenon from the simple, undeniable truth which lay so near to him, namely 'No object without a subject.'" If Kant had pushed his philosophy a few steps further, he would have arrived at the notion that "the object, because it always exists only in relation to a subject, is dependent thereon, is conditioned thereby, and is therefore mere phenomenon that does not exist in itself, does not exist unconditionally."[156] Though inaccessible, noumena remain related – or correlated – to phenomena, with the former tending to become increasingly subsumed within the latter. When pushed a bit further, one ends up with something that looks a lot like Idealism, with a metaphysical continuum between phenomena and noumena that promises to collapse Kant's split between them.

For Schopenhauer, Idealism can only overcome this split by dropping out one of the two terms – the noumena – thereby allowing a phenomenal monism to fill the gap. "All previous systems started either from the object or from the subject, and therefore sought to explain the one from the other, and this according to the principle of sufficient reason."[157] Idealism attempts to think a continuum between phenomena and noumena that is not reducible to either. But what it really ends up doing – in Schopenhauer's opinion – is adopting a partial view (that of subject and object) and universalizing this in the Absolute.

What, then, does Schopenhauer propose? One must re-examine not only the Kantian framework, but the basic presuppositions of the Idealist response to Kant. For Schopenhauer, the principle of sufficient reason is primary among these presuppositions that must be re-examined. For the pessimist philosopher, that "everything that exists, must exist for a reason" must not be taken for granted. But this leaves a great deal open, too much perhaps: What if there is no reason for the world's existence, either as phenomena or as noumena? What if the world-in-itself is not ordered, let alone ordered "for us"? What if the world-as-it-is, let alone the world-in-itself, is unintelligible, not in a relative way, but in an absolute way? Once one dispenses with the principle of sufficient reason, what is left – except a philosophy that can only be a non-philosophy? It would appear that two paths are left open – materialism or idealism, nihilism or mysticism, the hard facts and the great beyond, "it is what it is" and "there is something more..." As we will see, for Schopenhauer, pessimism is the only viable philosophical response to such an abandonment of the principle of sufficient reason.

Schopenhauer dismisses the Idealist response to Kant's phenomena-noumena split as inadequate. In its place he proposes a simple move – that Kant's split be re-cast in a way that allows for a collapse between them to take place. There is, first, the world as phenomena: "Everything that in any way belongs and can belong to the world is inevitably associated with this being-conditioned by the subject, and it exists only for the subject."[158] This includes the subject-object correlation, as well as the finer distinction that Schopenhauer later makes between the representation and the object of representation, both of which are contained within the world of phenomenon. Put simply, "the world is my representation."

Then there is, on the other side, the world as noumena, which is a pure limit that at once conditions thought and remains inaccessible to thought – "something to which no ground can ever be assigned, for which no explanation is possible, and no further cause is to be sought."[159] The concept of noumena can only ever be an apophatic concept. Schopenhauer enters deep waters here, not least because any attempt to conceptualize the noumenal world is doomed from the start. This never seems to deter the philosopher-curmudgeon, however. The challenge is how to think both the inaccessibility and the immanence of the world as noumena, and Schopenhauer glosses this via a concept of nothingness/emptiness that is at the same time not completely separate from the phenomenal world. One need not soar into the infinity of the cosmos or the inner depths of Spirit to discover such a concept. In *WWR* Schopenhauer discovers it in the mundane materiality of the body: "Thus it happens that to everyone the thing-in-itself is known immediately in so far as it appears as his own body, and only mediately in so far as it is objectified in the other objects of perception."[160] What results is a strange immanentism of noumena: the correlation of subject and object that constitutes phenomena is the world considered as representation (*Vorstellung*), and that which is absolutely inaccessible to this world-as-representation, but which is also inseparable from it, is the world considered as will (*Wille*). "[T]he world is, on the one side, entirely representation, just as, on the other, it is entirely will."[161]

* * *

Schopenhauer and the Negation of Life. Like his Idealist contemporaries, Schopenhauer agrees that "Kant's greatest merit is the distinction of the phenomenon from the thing-in-itself."[162] And like his contemporaries Schopenhauer views this distinction as something to be overcome. But whereas the Idealist response is to adopt an ontology of generosity to bridge this gap, Schopenhauer will adopt a different approach. Instead of asserting an Absolute Life (grounded by its own principle of sufficiency, and driven by an ontology of overpresence),

Schopenhauer will drop the bottom out of the ontology of generosity. What remains is, quite simply, nothing. No overflowing life force, no pantheistic becoming, no immanent principle of life running throughout all of Creation. Just nothing. But nothing is, of course, never simple; it is also nothingness, or emptiness, or the void, and it quickly becomes a paradoxical and enigmatic something. So while Schopenhauer does not definitively resolve the Kantian problematic, he does provide a way of shifting the entire orientation of thought on the problem.

The new problem Schopenhauer is confronted with is how to overcome the Kantian split between phenomena and noumena, but without being determined by the ontology of generosity. This can be stated in even briefer terms: how to think "life" such that it is not always determined by overpresence (that is, by generosity, genesis, and givenness); *how to think life in terms of negation.* Certainly one would not want to return to a metaphysics of life, in which life obtains the quality of pure being that one finds in the concept of "soul," common to both Aristotle and Aquinas. But Schopenhauer is equally skeptical of the diffuse theism in the Idealist notions of the Absolute, in which Absolute Life always radiates and flows forth, often finding its culmination in the heights of human life in particular. Schopenhauer notes, with some sarcasm, "life is thus given as a gift, whence it is evident that anyone would have declined it with thanks had he looked at it and tested it beforehand."[163]

The remaining option for Schopenhauer is to consider the role that negation plays in relation to any ontology of life, especially any ontology of life that would attempt to overcome the Kantian split of phenomena and noumena. Life, then, is not simply subordinate to a metaphysics of presence (as in Kant), but neither is it consonant with an infinite overpresence of generosity (as with Idealism). In contrast to the ontology of generosity, which posits life as always affirmative, Schopenhauer will put forth a negative ontology, in which life is paradoxically grounded in nothingness (it is, perhaps, "underpresent"). In a striking turn of phrase, Schopenhauer refers to all these relations between negation and life as the Will-to-Life (*Wille zum Leben*):

> As the will is the thing-in-itself, the inner content, the essence of the world, but life, the visible world, the phenomenon, is only the mirror of the will, this world will accompany the will as inseparably as a body is accompanied by its shadow; and if will exists, then life, the world, will exist. Therefore life is certain to the will-to-live...[164]

Schopenhauer's concept of the Will-to-Life is a response to an old dilemma concerning the ontology of life. It is found in Aristotle, and then in natural philosophy, before its recapitulation in Kant. We have seen it at play in German Idealism, in the ontology of generosity and its affirmative overpresence. Put simply, the dilemma is how to articulate a concept of life-in-itself that would account for all the instances of the living. If one is to avoid both the naïveté of epistemological classification, as well as the rhetorical games of nominalism, what is required is a concept of life that is at once synonymous with the living, and yet transcendentally separated from it.

The Will-to-Life is, then, Schopenhauer's attempt to overcome the Kantian split by asserting a subtractive continuity, a continuity paradoxically driven by negation. At the same time, sentences such as those in the citation above demand some unpacking, since in order to arrive at his concept of the Will-to-Life, Schopenhauer must make a number of steps (steps which many of his critics perceived as fallacious or untenable). With this in mind, we can briefly consider the three aspects of the Will-to-Life as presented by Schopenhauer in *WWR*.

* * *

The Riddle of Life. Early on in *WWR* Schopenhauer recasts the Kantian problematic through the example of the living body. His concern, however, is neither a "body" in the sense of physics, which would commit him to mechanism or atomism, nor "body" in the sense of biology, which would commit him to natural philosophy. Instead the body is for Schopenhauer a kind of crystallization of abstract anonymity, a "Will" that is at once energy and drive, but that has no origin or end, and leads to no goal. The body is that which is the most familiar and yet the most foreign to us as subjects. We are bodies, and we have bodies.[165] For Schopenhauer these are simply two ways of knowing the body – immediately as a living subject consonant with a living body, and mediately as a subject relating to or thinking about the body as object. Both of these are well within the domain of the phenomenal world that Kant describes.

But in the Second Book of *WWR* Schopenhauer will take Kant a step further. If the body, as both subject and object, is on the side of the world as phenomena (as representation), then what would the living body as a thing-in-itself be? If there is a phenomena of life, is there also a noumena of life, a life-in-itself? On the one hand, such a noumenal life could not be something completely divorced from life as phenomenal, for then there would be no point of connection between phenomena and noumena (a logical prerequisite for Kant). On the other hand, this noumenal life must retain a minimal equivocity with regard to phenomenal life, else we are simply back within the phenomenal domain of subject-object relations.

Hence Schopenhauer's riddle of life: what is that through which life is at once the nearest and the farthest, the most familiar and the most strange? As Schopenhauer notes, "the answer to the riddle is given to the subject of knowledge appearing as individual, and this answer is given in the word *Will*."[166] The Will is, in Schopenhauer's hands, that which is common to subject and object, but not reducible to either. This Will is never present in itself, either as subjective experience or as objective knowledge; it necessarily remains a negative manifestation. Indeed, Schopenhauer will press this further, suggesting that "the whole body is nothing but objectified will, i.e., will that has become representation."[167] And again: "My body and will are one... or, My body is the *objectivity* of my will."[168]

In reply to the riddle "what is nearest and farthest?" Schopenhauer answers with the Will – that which is fully immanent and yet absolutely inaccessible. As we noted, Schopenhauer's first step is to re-cast Kant's framework in new terms – for Kantian phenomena he will use the term Representation, and for Kantian noumena he will use the term Will. His next step is to describe the living body, and more specifically life, as the nexus where Will and Representation meet. Schopenhauer's reply is that to each instance of the world taken as Representation there is the world as Will; and to each instance of life as Representation (whether as subject or object), there is a correlative Will-to-Life:

> The will, considered purely in itself, is devoid of knowledge, and is only a blind, irresistible urge, as we see it appear in inorganic and vegetable nature... and as what the will wills is always life, just because this is nothing but the presentation of that willing for the representation, it is immaterial and a mere pleonasm if, instead of simply saying "the will," we say "the will-to-life."[169]

Certainly life obtains a duality within the domain of Representation – there is the subjective experience of living, just as there is the scientific knowledge of the living, both inscribed within the world as Representation or phenomena. Schopenhauer's controversial move here is to assert that there is life outside of and apart from the world as Representation, that there is a life which remains inaccessible to the phenomenon of life, and his phrase Will-to-Life designates this horizon.

* * *

Life Negating Life. However, at this point, the problem is that Schopenhauer appears to have only elevated the concept of life beyond ontology, to the realm of unthinkable noumena. There still remains a part of the riddle to be answered, which is how that which is nearest can – *at the same time* – be that which is farthest. For this the role of negation in the Will-to-Life becomes more important.

Schopenhauer notes that the Will is not simply a static, transcendent category of being, but a dynamic, continuous principle that is much in line with Idealist concept of the Absolute. But, as we've seen, Schopenhauer distances himself from Idealism by opposing the ontology of generosity that it puts forth.[170] As Schopenhauer comments, "everywhere we see contest, struggle, and the fluctuation of victory, and... we shall recognize in this more distinctly that variance with itself essential to the will."[171] Schopenhauer provides a veritable compendium of examples from the sciences, though they read more like scenes from a monster movie: insects that lay their eggs in the bodies of other host insects, for whom birth is death; the internalized predator-prey relationship in the hydra; the ant whose head and tail fight each other if the body is cut in two; invasive species such as ivy; giant oak trees whose branches become so intertwined that the tree suffocates. His examples continue, up through the cosmic negation of black holes, down to the basic chemical decomposition of matter in the decay of corpses, where life is defined by the negation of life.

Yet Schopenhauer is neither a Hobbes nor a Darwin; his emphasis here is less on the universalizing of struggle, and more on what it indicates for an ontology of life. If the Will is flow or a continuum, it is, for Schopenhauer, one driven by negation – or by a negative flow, a negative continuum. The Will asserts itself through contradictions, oppositions, subtractions, and its limit is the self-negation of life, through life. Thus "the will-to-live (*Wille zum Leben*) generally feasts on itself, and is in different forms its own nourishment, until finally the human race, because it subdues all the others, regards nature as manufactured for its own use."[172]

For Schopenhauer, there is an "inner antagonism" to the Will, one that is antagonistic at the level of this or that living being, as well as in the domain of inorganic nature, on through to the level of cosmic life. The Will-to-Life is driven by this process of "life negating life," from the inorganic to the organic and beyond.

* * *

Cosmic Pessimism. In the inner antagonism of the Will-to-Life Schopenhauer comes upon what is perhaps his greatest insight, and that is its radically unhuman aspect. Schopenhauer here pulls apart the Kantian split, suggesting that all claims concerning noumena are necessarily compromised by concepts derived in some way from the phenomenal domain. And it is here that Schopenhauer most directly counters the furtive anthropocentrism in post-Kantian Idealism. In the same way that the domain of noumena does not exist for phenomena, so the Will-to-Life is utterly indifferent to any concept of life, be it "for us" or "in itself." In the Will-to-Life "we see at the very lowest grade the will manifesting itself as a blind impulse, an obscure, dull urge, remote from all direct knowableness."[173]

In statements like these, Schopenhauer is actually making two separate claims. The first has to do with the principle of sufficient reason, and Schopenhauer's critical treatment of it. In so far as the Will-to-Life is noumenal as well as phenomenal, all statements concerning its causality, its teleology, its relation to time and space, and its logical coherence or intelligibility, must only apply within the phenomenal domain. In this sense "the will as thing-in-itself lies outside the province of the principle of sufficient reason in all its forms, and is consequently completely groundless, although each of its phenomena is entirely subject to that principle."[174] Schopenhauer admits that one can always recuperate any and all statements about the Will into the phenomenal domain, a recuperative move in which one is still able to articulate that which is inarticulable, to think that which is unthinkable. But in this paradoxical mode there is always something for which, taken in itself, no sufficient reason can suffice, or for which there is only a negation of sufficient reason. We might even say that Schopenhauer's concept of the Will-to-Life ultimately points to a principle of *insufficient* reason at its core.

If the Will-to-Life, considered in itself, has no sufficient reason because it lies outside the phenomenal domain, so can the Will-to-Life not be granted any anthropocentric conceits, least of all that life exists "for us" as human beings, or that it reaches its pinnacle in the human life. Like his German contemporaries, Schopenhauer posits a principle of continuity that would collapse the Kantian split between phenomena and noumena; but unlike them, he refuses to grant the human being, or the human perspective, any priority with respect to this principle. Certainly, as Schopenhauer readily admits, there are gradations and differentiations within the natural world. What remains, however, is this Will-to-Life that indifferently cuts across them all. "For it is indeed one and the same will that objectifies itself in the whole world; it knows no time, for that form of the principle of sufficient reason does not belong to it, or to its original objectivity, namely the Ideas, but only to the way in which these are known by the individuals who are themselves transitory..."[175]

Even as it is rendered hierarchical for Schopenhauer, the Will-to-Life maintains this cosmic indifference throughout the world. Indeed, Schopenhauer will go so far as to say that this constitutes the tragic-comic character of human life in particular: "The life of every individual, viewed as a whole and in general, and when only its most significant features are emphasized, is really a tragedy; but gone through in detail it has the character of a comedy."[176]

For Schopenhauer, pessimism is the only viable philosophical response to this radically unhuman condition. This pessimism is something for which Schopenhauer is popularly known (and often dismissed). The problem is that Schopenhauer's pessimism is often understood to be about human life, for it is only human beings that sense the senselessness and suffering of the world. It is true that Schopenhauer's pessimism has to do with a view of life as essentially "incurable suffering and endless misery," an ongoing cycle of suffering and boredom. But this is only the case from the perspective of the individual, living subject, towards which, for Schopenhauer, the world-in-itself is indifferent. As Schopenhauer evocatively notes, every manifestation of the Will-to-Life is doubled by a kind of Willlessness (*Willenslosigkeit*), every sense of the world-for-us doubled by a world-without-us. Pessimism for Schopenhauer is not so much an individual, personal attitude, but really a cosmic one – an impersonal attitude. The indifference of the Will-to-Life thus stretches from the micro-scale to the macro-scale:

> Thus everyone in this twofold regard is the whole world itself, the microcosm; he finds its two sides whole and complete within himself. And what he thus recognizes as his own inner being also exhausts the inner being of the whole world, the macrocosm. Thus the whole world, like man himself, is through and through will and through and through representation, and beyond this there is nothing.[177]

In an enigmatic way, negation courses through Schopenhauer's notion of the Will-to-Life. Evocations of the Will-to-Life as "nothing" or "nothingness" recur throughout Schopenhauer's writings. Certainly Schopenhauer was influenced by his encounter with classical texts in the Buddhist traditions.[178] As we've noted, this type of cosmic pessimism stands in opposition to the ontology of generosity in post-Kantian Idealism, with its emphasis on overpresence, flux and flow, and the becoming of the Absolute. In response to the Kantian split between Life and the living, and in contrast to the post-Kantian ontology of generosity, Schopenhauer opts for a negative ontology of life.

However, that life is "nothing" can mean several things. The enigmatic last section of *WWR I* bears out some of these meanings. Here Schopenhauer makes use of Kant's distinction between two kinds of nothing: the *nihil privativum* or privative nothing, and the *nihil negativum* or negative nothing. The former is nothing defined as the absence of something (e.g. shadow as absence of light, death as absence of life). For Schopenhauer the world is nothing in this privative sense as this interplay between Representation and Will; the world, with all its subject-object relations, as well as its ongoing suffering and boredom, is transitory and ephemeral. By contrast, the indifferent Will-to-Life courses through and cuts across it all, whilst remaining in itself inaccessible, and "nothing."

The problem is that, at best, we have limited and indirect access to the world as a *nihil privativum*, and "so long as we ourselves are the will-to-live, this last, namely the nothing as that which exists, can be known and expressed by us only negatively."[179] For Schopenhauer the very fact that there is no getting outside the world of the *nihil privativum* hints at a further negation, one that is not a relative but an absolute nothingness. As he notes, "in opposition to this *nihil privativum*, the *nihil negativum* has been set up, which would in every respect be nothing." But this is not simple opposition, for "a really proper *nihil negativum* is not even conceivable" but is, in the end "always only a *nihil privativum*."[180]

At this point it seems that one must say – or think – nothing more. It is as if philosophy ultimately leads to its own negation, to Wittgenstein's claim that what cannot be thought must be passed over in silence. That *WWR* closes with an enigmatic affirmation of life as nothingness is indicative of the limits of Schopenhauer's negative ontology. On the one hand the Will-to-Life is nothingness because, considered as the interplay between Life and the living, the Will-to-Life in itself is never something in an affirmative or positive sense. But Schopenhauer suggests that the Will-to-Life is nothingness for a further reason, which is that, in itself, the Will-to-Life indicates that which is never manifest, that which is never an objectification of the Will, that which is never a Will for a Representation. To the relative nothingness of the *nihil privativum* there is the absolute nothingness (*absolutes Nichts*) of the *nihil negativum*. While Schopenhauer is himself opposed to the post-Kantian Idealists, he is united with them in his interest in the concept of the Absolute, albeit one paradoxically grounded in nothingness. His contribution is to have thought the Absolute without resorting to the ontology of generosity and its undue reliance on romantic conceptions of Life, Nature, and the human. It is for this reason that Schopenhauer can close *WWR I* by stating that "this very real world of ours with all its suns and galaxies, is – nothing."[181]

* * *

Philosophical Doomcore. All of this leads to a deceptively simple question: do pessimists have an ethics? If they do, do they always expect the worst outcome, even in the face of well-intentioned actions? For that matter, wouldn't the true pessimist be unethical, precisely in the sense that they themselves would be incapable of any effective action? The problem is that pessimists still *do* things, even if all they do is complain. This is the double bind of a pessimist ethics – decision without efficacy, acting without believing, the abiding sense that, ultimately, everything will turn out for the worst, all will be for naught.

An oft-cited example in this regard is Voltaire's 18th century satire *Candide; or, Optimism*. Candide, an impressionable youth living a life free of worry, is educated according to the Enlightenment values of rational self-reliance by his teacher, Pangloss. Candide holds steadfast to the Panglossian motto that everything will turn out for the best, since this is the best of all possible worlds. But as Candide grows into adulthood, he is confronted by one situation after another that challenges this view, until it becomes absurd for Candide to continue to assert that everything turns out for the best. Disillusioned and confused, the narrative ends with Candide retreating into the solipsistic attitude of each person "tending their own garden," the question of whether this is indeed the best of all possible worlds left open.[182]

But Candide is not just a pessimist, he is also a part of the European Enlightenment's roving band of do-gooders. In other words, even though he becomes more and more disillusioned, Candide goes along with things all the same. He does not leave the culture he is a part of, he does not shut himself up in a desert cave, and he does not enjoy his solitude and write existential meditations on the virtues of suicide. Of course, there may be an eminently practical reason for this: to whom could Candide complain if he were alone? Yet nobody wants to hear such complaints. In a sense, Candide's growing confusion, along with Pangloss' absurd optimism, are challenges to the ethical world view in which Voltaire's narrative takes place – that there is good and evil, that the difference between them can be discerned, that action can be moral and have moral effects, that the "healthy" attitude for any adventurer in life is to be positive and try your best, that life is "out there" to be lived.

At first glance, Schopenhauer – that arch-pessimist of philosophers – presents a similar case. Judging by his rather curmudgeonly outlook, it would appear that for Schopenhauer, ethics would be about as necessary to philosophy as self-consciousness to a stone. In fact, Schopenhauer often cited an analogy borrowed from Spinoza: if a stone thrown through the air were conscious, it would fancy that it moved itself through the air of its own will and of its own accord.

Until recently, readers would have had to look to Schopenhauer's magnum opus, *The World as Will and Representation*, for anything like a pessimist ethics. In it one would find statements here and there about the suffering of the world, about how it is better not to have been born at all, and so on. But there is little in the way of a sustained, critical examination of the topic.[183] This is where Schopenhauer's work in *The Two Fundamental Problems of Ethics* comes into play. It comprises two long essays by Schopenhauer written several years after *WWR*. The ethics essays not only build upon this latter work, but they also isolate a fascinating lacuna within Schopenhauer's darkly cosmic metaphysics – in a world bereft of foundation or meaning, a world constituted by an indifferent, inhuman "Will," how should one act? Given that the world is indifferent, what should one do?

Schopenhauer published *The Two Fundamental Problems of Ethics* in book form in 1841. However the two texts in it were originally submitted to essay competitions. The first competition was hosted by the Royal Norwegian Society of Sciences, for which Schopenhauer submitted his essay "On the Freedom of the Human Will." The second competition was hosted by the Royal Danish Society of Sciences, for which Schopenhauer wrote the essay "On the Basis of Morals." To his delight, Schopenhauer was awarded the top prize for the first essay.

Delight soon gave way to chagrin, however, in the case of the second essay. Schopenhauer was the only person to submit an essay, and yet the Royal Danish Society refused to grant him a prize – or for that matter, any recognition at all. They pretended he didn't exist. To add insult to injury, in their comments on Schopenhauer's essay, the Royal Danish Society members would also reference "distinguished philosophers" such as Hegel. One can only imagine the absurdity of the situation for the pessimist from Danzig. When Schopenhauer published both essays in book form in 1841, he made sure to note that the second essay was "not awarded a prize," and added lengthy retorts and rants against the Royal Danish Society's comments on the essay. He would also make incisive remarks concerning "journal writers sworn to the glorification of the bad," of "paid professors of Hegelry," of Hegel's philosophy as a "colossal mystification that will provide even posterity with the inexhaustible theme of ridiculing our age," and of German Idealism generally as a "pseudo-philosophy that cripples all mental powers."

Fisticuffs aside, it is important to note that in the case of both essays, Schopenhauer was in effect prompted to write about ethics; he was prompted by the announcement of the competition itself, but also by the particular questions to which contestants were to reply. The questions posed by the organisers in each case provides Schopenhauer with something to push against, and I would argue that it is this kind of philosophical resistance in his writing that makes *The Two Fundamental Problems of Ethics* still relevant today.

In the first prize essay, the question (originally posed in scholarly Latin) was, "Can the freedom of the human will be proved from self-consciousness?" For the second prize essay, the question, this time longer and more opaque, was, "Is the source and basis of morals to be sought in an idea of morality that resides in consciousness, and in an analysis of the remaining basic moral concepts that arise out of it, or in another cognitive ground?" To both questions Schopenhauer answers in the negative. No, he says, the human will is free only insofar as the ground of human will is free – that is, only insofar as a more fundamental, abstract, and non-human Will is free. For the second question Schopenhauer also answers no, and he even goes so far as to question the presumption that human morality has anything to do with reason at all, choosing to instead explore the concept of compassion (*Mitleid*) and the vaguely Eastern notion of loving kindness (*Menschenliebe*) as the basis for morality.

In *WWR* Schopenhauer had attempted to radicalize Kant, presenting a two-sided view of the world. On the one hand the phenomenal world of appearances, bodies, objects and nature – the world of Representation; on the other hand, that which grounds that phenomenal world, but which is itself not any Representation, and is instead an anonymous, indifferent, blind striving – the world of Will. Schopenhauer remained convinced that, even though the world as Will remained inaccessible to us as human beings in the world of Representation, there was a connection between them, particularly in the living body. The body and life were, for Schopenhauer, this nexus of the Will in Representation, of an undifferentiated Will in an individuated human will, of the non-human in the human.

While this would seem to steer things inevitably towards an ethical philosophy, *WWR* does something altogether different. It is, of course, concerned with the human world and the human capacity for making sense of the world, but by the funereal fourth book of *WWR*, ethics drops away in favor of discussions on mysticism, Eastern philosophy, pessimism and the enigmatic idea of not-willing or "Willlessness." To be more precise, *The Two Fundamental Problems of Ethics* highlights a gap within *WWR* – how to connect the indifferent and inhuman world of Will with the all-too-human world of Representation?

In the first essay – "On the Freedom of the Will" – Schopenhauer breaks down the long-standing debate in ethical philosophy over freedom and necessity. He distinguishes between different types of freedom (physical, intellectual, and moral), arguing that freedom is essentially a negative concept, the absence or removal of an obstacle to action. Schopenhauer's primary target is the illusion of purely self-conscious acts, the presumption that freedom derives directly from willing (the notion that, as Schopenhauer says, "I am free if I can do what I will"). But what grounds this isomorphism of freedom and will? As Schopenhauer notes, one would have to inquire not just into the doing based on willing, but the willing of the willing of doing, and so on. One either follows this question to infinity, or one must presume a paradoxical groundless ground, a Will for all willing that does not itself will anything.

Likewise, Schopenhauer distinguishes three types of necessity (logical, mathematical, and physical). While he maintains the freedom-necessity pair, he also attempts to show that they can only be properly related outside the sphere of the human subject. If, as Schopenhauer argues, freedom is a negative concept, then it is also the absence of necessity. But the absence of necessity, taken to its logical conclusion, entails a notion of "absolute contingency": "So the free, as absence of necessity is its distinguishing mark, would have to be that which simply depended on no cause whatsoever, and would have to be defined as *absolutely contingent*; a highly problematical concept, whose thinkability I do not vouch for, but which in a strange way coincides with that of *freedom*."[184] Passages like these betray, in an interesting way, Schopenhauer's ongoing ambiguity surrounding ethics – particularly the investment of good faith in the human that Schopenhauer thinks he needs in order to think about ethics at all. In an analogy he develops later on, Schopenhauer likens the human being's bloated over-reliance on free will and choice to being as absurd as a self-conscious pool of water: "That is exactly as if water were to speak: I can strike up high waves (yes! in the sea and storm), I can rush down in a hurry (yes! in the bed of a stream), I can fall down foaming and spraying (yes! in a fountain)... and yet I am doing none of that now, but I am staying with free will calm and clear in the mirroring pond."[185]

If the first essay is primarily concerned with critiquing the individuationist and humanist notion of ethical action (freedom vs. necessity), then the second essay – "On the Basis of Morality" – tackles the broader question of the ground of ethics itself. It is no wonder Schopenhauer was not granted a prize for this essay – from the start he contentiously implies the stupidity of the question, while also noting the "exuberant difficulty" of the problem of grounds. Here Schopenhauer's target is Kant; but his extended critique of Kant is also laced with admiration. As Schopenhauer notes, Kant's greatest contribution to ethical philosophy was to tear it away from *eudaimonia* (happiness, well-being). Whereas for the ancients virtue and happiness were identical, for the moderns virtue and happiness are related as ground and result. The axiomatic approach of Kant focuses less on *eudaimonia* and more on the practical aspect of ethical action. But here Schopenhauer is quite critical, for Kant's categorical imperative, with its emphasis on the "ought," can only lead to the absurd idea of a totalising "ought": "In a practical philosophy we have to do not with providing grounds for what happens but rather laws for what *ought to happen even if it never does*... Who tells you that *what never happens ought to happen?*"[186]

In short, Schopenhauer sees in Kant's categorical imperative a church masquerading as a court of law: "Conceiving ethics in an *imperative* form, as *doctrine of duty*, and thinking of the moral worth or unworthiness of human actions as fulfilment or dereliction of *duties*, undeniably stems, together with the *ought*, solely from theological morals, and in turn from the Decalogue."[187] Schopenhauer later riffs on Kant's ethics as having a mystical, "hyperphysical" core: "...in the Kantian school practical reason with its categorical imperative appears as a hyperphysical fact, as a Delphic temple in the human mind, from whose murky sanctuary oracular utterances announce without fail not, unfortunately, what *will* happen, but what *ought* to happen."[188]

And here we see Schopenhauer directly attempting to build a bridge between the ontological claims of *WWR* and the ethical claims of *The Two Fundamental Problems of Ethics*. The upshot of this, as Schopenhauer chooses to state with some subtlety, is that "in this the human being is no exception to the rest of nature."[189] That is, insofar as freedom is impersonal and unhuman, the human is simply part of a larger field that is at once metaphysical and ethical. Paradoxically, Schopenhauer's thinking moves towards something we can only call an *unhuman ethics*.

Of course, the major challenge is how to re-conceive of ethics given this unhuman metaphysics. In the second essay Schopenhauer gives us hints of such an ethics, setting up two pairs of ethical concepts: the poles of self-oriented action and other-oriented action, and the poles of well-being and woe. From this he derives his two key "positive" concepts that close the essay: that of compassion (*Mitleid*) and that of loving-kindness (*Menschenliebe*). He shifts the debate away from the preoccupation with human reason and law.

At the same time, his discussion on compassion remains open-ended; one senses that for Schopenhauer compassion is not limited to the feeling of one human being for another, but that it can be open to perhaps strange, unhuman compassions – with the animal, the plant, the rock, the ocean, the cloud, the swarm, the number, the concept, or what have you. Such compassions, such instances of "suffering-with," can range from sentiments of dread and horror to sentiments of affinity and the loss of self. Similarly, Schopenhauer's ever-eccentric appropriation of Eastern thought, and his concept of loving-kindness is not simply a love of the human for the human, but quite the opposite – one loves the human only as a starting point for loving the unhuman.

* * *

Better Not to Be. In spite of his misgivings vis-à-vis humanity, it is important to note that Schopenhauer's pessimism is of a particular type. In general pessimism can be characterized by one of several statements. One version is of the type "this is the worst of all possible worlds." Essentially an inversion of the optimistic view, in this view any possible positive in the world is always outweighed by a negative; indeed, the very fact that there is a negative at all (that we are mortal, that we suffer, or that we are fated to die) trumps any possible positive.

Another version of pessimism comes in the statement that "life is not worth living." A result, in a way, of the first statement – the worst of all possible worlds – this view transcribes a statement about the world to a statement about the subject "thrown" into that world. If this is the worst of all possible worlds, then the value of what it means to live in that world can only be matched by an equal pessimism of life, be it bare biological life or the qualified life of self-conscious beings. Indeed, in this view it is precisely due to consciousness that pessimism, as a viewpoint, exists at all.

Yet another version of pessimism presents an even more austere statement: "it is better not to be." The first statement – this is the worst of all possible worlds – asserts something about the world as such. The second statement – life is not worth living – shifts the focus to the subject living in such a world. This statement – it is better not to be – shifts the focus again to the metaphysical plane, encompassing as it does both the world and the fact of living in the world. It expands the pessimist's misanthropy beyond humanity to all existing things, living or non-living, physical or metaphysical. In this view it is *being itself* that is the problem, not some property of the world or of the human being.

Each of these statements, though it makes strong assertions, is also compromised by loopholes in logic that undermine those assertions. For instance, the pessimist statement "this is the worst of all possible worlds" tends to conflate a state of the world with a judgment about the state of the world. Hence pessimism holds a tenuous position within philosophy, caught somewhere between a logical axiom and a bad attitude. In addition, though it rails against life, against humanity, and against existence itself, pessimism must always make such assertions from the point of view of the living, existing, human subject. Hence its negations against life, against the human, and against being itself are also evocations of the non-human, of non-being or nothingness. And, as such, they remain horizons for the pessimist. They are negations that in themselves cannot be thought as such. Here we are brought to a central insight concerning pessimism – that it "fails," and that, in a way, it must fail. The pinnacle of pessimist logic, carried to its extreme, is the undermining of the pessimist project itself.

We can qualify this further, paying particular attention to pessimism not just as a "bad attitude" but as a philosophical position – tenuous though it is. In the history of philosophy, pessimism is generally split between two views: a moral pessimism and a metaphysical pessimism.[190] In moral pessimism, one expresses an attitude about the world that takes the worst possible view of things. The moral pessimist at his or her height can take any phenomenon, no matter how apparently joyful, beneficial, or happy, and turn it into the worst possible scenario (even if only to note that every positive only paves the way for a negative). This is the typical view of the glass being half-empty. Note that moral pessimism is pessimistic because its view is pessimistic, irrespective of what is happening in the world. The tendency to take the worst view of things, or the tendency to always expect the worst, is about an interpretation of the world, not about the world in itself.

This changes once one moves from moral pessimism to metaphysical pessimism. In the former one expresses an attitude about the world, whereas in the latter one makes claims about the world itself. This is the view that it is the objective property of every glass in itself to be partially empty. Metaphysical pessimism is more than just a bad attitude, it makes claims about the way in which the world in itself is structured or ordered. For the metaphysical pessimist, the world itself is ordered in the worst possible way and is structured such that it always leads to the worst possible ends. For the metaphysical pessimist, saying that this is the worst of all possible worlds is less a case of being grumpy and more a statement about the radical antagonism between the world itself and our wants and desires.

While Schopenhauer expresses both of these types of pessimism, he remains dissatisfied with both, for both rely on a stable division between a human subject and a non-human world within which the subject is embedded. The only difference is that with moral pessimism, we have a subjective attitude about the worst of all possible worlds, and with metaphysical pessimism we have an objective claim about the worst of all possible worlds. But both views, being concerned with "the worst" (*pessimus*), implicitly rely on an anthropocentric view – either one is stuck with a bad attitude or one is stuck in a bad world. (As Sid Waterman once put it, "I see the glass half full, but full of poison.")

So, while Schopenhauer himself was a curmudgeon, and while he does state that this is the worst of all possible worlds, his philosophy ultimately moves towards a third type of pessimism, one that he never names but which we have tenuously christened a *cosmic pessimism*.[191] For Schopenhauer, the logical endpoint of pessimism is to question the self-world dichotomy that enables pessimism to exist at all. But such a move would entail a shift away from the relation and difference between self and world, human and non-human, subjective attitude and objective claim. Instead, it would entail a move towards an *indifference*, an indifference of the world toward the self, even of the self toward the self. Cosmic pessimism would therefore question even the misanthropy of moral and metaphysical pessimism, for even this leaves us as human beings with a residual consolation – at least the world cares enough to be "against" us. Schopenhauer's cosmic pessimism questions ethical philosophy's principle of sufficient reason – that there is an inherent order to the world that is the ground that enables reliable judgements to be made regarding moral and ethical action. It also questions the fundamental relation between ethics and action, whether of the Aristotelian first principles type, the Kantian-axiomatic type, or the modern cognitivist-affectivist type. Cosmic pessimism seems to move towards an uncanny zone of passivity, "letting be," even a kind of liminal quietism in which non-being is the main category. In cosmic pessimism, this "indifference" is the horizon of all ethics. As an ethics, this is, surely, absurd. And this is perhaps why Schopenhauer's ethics ultimately "fails."

Despite their different orientations, *WWR* and *The Two Fundamental Problems of Ethics* are united by a common approach, and that is an inversion of metaphysics and ethics. Schopenhauer tends to begin with human experience, even and especially if that experience is one that mitigates against the illusory coherence of the subject. All of Schopenhauer's rants concerning pessimism and the limits of human knowledge dovetail on this strange counter-experience, the experience that the subject is not a subject, the experience of the dissolving of the *principum individuationis*. Part of Schopenhauer's strategy is to undo the notion that the subject is separate from the world it experiences, that it relates to, and that it produces knowledge about. Part of his strategy is also to prod the notion, which he inherits from Kant, that there is an inaccessible, unknowable, noumenal world "in itself" from which we are forever barred access. Both of these issues deal with the problematic category of the human – the human being as living in a human-centric world, accessible or not, that always exists "for us" as human beings.

The question of ethics becomes especially pertinent here.

Schopenhauer's essays refuse relying on either the human individual or the group as its foundation, much less any discussion on human nature, the state of nature, or what have you. Schopenhauer also refuses relying on either intuition (or any innate, moral faculty) or law (as in the axiomatism of Kant). Instead, Schopenhauer zooms-out from the traditional, humanist ethical discourse to the larger issues of ethics as the self-world relation – or, really, ethics as the impossibility of this relation. In fact, while Schopenhauer does not go this far, I am tempted to suggest that *The Two Fundamental Problems of Ethics*, when read alongside *WWR*, poses the problem of *an ethics without the human*. Given our current concerns with climate change and global disasters, the time would seem ripe for an exploration into such an ethics. But an unhuman ethics would have to avoid both the pole of an all-too-human ethics (in which ethics takes place exclusively and solely within the spheres of law and policy), and the pole of a romantic ethics (in which the ethics of animals or the environment presumes a naïve notion of nature).

The Two Fundamental Problems of Ethics puts forth some key philosophical points that resonate deeply with our so-called posthuman era. The first is that Schopenhauer displaces the ethical discourse of free will by externalizing human will as an unhuman Will. He does this through a questioning of the basis of human will and his negative concept of freedom. Though he does not name the anonymous, abstract Will as such, his critique of the human-ethical subject points in this direction. And this leads to another point, which is that Schopenhauer constantly shifts the scale of his discussion of ethics beyond the human institutions of religion, law or politics. This is a contentious point, for, as Schopenhauer well knows, this non-human aspect of the world can never be proved as such (nor would any such proof prove anything). But in his criticisms of the traditional terms of ethical philosophy, one senses Schopenhauer's ontological commitment to some metaphysical principle in excess of the human. And it is here that *The Two Fundamental Problems of Ethics* comes into focus. Schopenhauer does not divide the unhuman Will from the human, all-too-human will, but is constantly at pains to show their immanence to each other, the Will in the will (or Will-in-will), as it were. The individuated human being is what he wills, but this will is also the Will, the human also the unhuman.

* * *

Logics of the Worst. Pessimism is based on a negation, encapsulated in its root term, "the worst." In saying that this is the worst of all possible worlds, or that life is not worth living, or that it is better not to be, pessimism takes something existent presumed to have value – the world, life, being – and negates its value. When it does this, it is also implying that what we presume to have a substantial existence (and hence value) in fact does not have a substantial existence (and this applies even to existence itself). The world, life, even being itself is without value, and their existence as arbitrary as anything else.

Where pessimist logic often gets caught is between a negation that states that something has a negative value, and a negation that states that something has no value. The first is an oppositional negation, a minus for every plus in the balance sheet of life, the world, existence itself. The second is a nullifying negation, a flattening of value systems themselves, which would argue back and forth interminably about the value or valuelessness of the world, life, and being. The first says that the world is not meaningful but meaningless, not joyful but sad, not good but evil, and so forth. The second says that the world is neither meaningful nor meaningless, neither good nor evil, neither joyful nor sad, neither this nor that.

So-called pessimist philosophers often waver between these two negations. Schopenhauer, for instance, will at one point sardonically note that if we asked the dead in their graves whether they would like to live again, they would surely shake their heads. Their pessimism is based on their experience, the balance sheet of life tipping towards the negative. But at other points Schopenhauer's thought will move towards the nullification of all terms, towards "Willlessness," the quietism of neutralized being, the silence of self-negating thought.

Let us try to refine this further. The logic of pessimism is structured around two qualitative statements. One is a statement on metaphysics, which makes a claim about the world, life, or even being as such. A breach exists between the self and the world in which the self finds itself, a gap between the world as it exists for us and in relation to us (the world-for-us) and the world as it is exists in itself, apart from our relating to it (the world-in-itself). Can this breach be crossed? For a philosopher like Kant, the answer is no, for we as human beings are always embedded in the world, always sensing, intuiting, and apprehending the world as sensory and cognitive subjects. By contrast, German Idealist philosophers assert that yes, this breach can be traversed, by virtue of the fact that we as human beings are part of the world, and that the world-in-itself is also "in" us. For German Idealism, the for-us *is* the in-itself. The concept of the Absolute comes to signify this equivalence.

For his part, Schopenhauer sides with Kant, but his reasons are slightly different. True, there is an irrevocable gap between self and world, and, even though we as human beings are part of the world, we forget that the world is not human. As such, to presume to gain knowledge of the world also presumes that there is an order hidden "out there" in the world to be revealed. But for Schopenhauer this is pure vanity – there is literally *no reason* that the world should be ordered in this way or that, or ordered at all. What both Kant and German Idealism presume is, using Aristotle's terms, a principle of sufficient reason that governs both the world-for-us and the world-in-itself.

Schopenhauer, though he is in many respects a died-in-the-wool Kantian, holds no such illusions.

Tied to this statement on metaphysics is another, a statement on humanism. It follows from the statement on metaphysics. Can this breach between self and world be crossed? If so, can it be crossed by human beings? Are human beings uniquely situated to traverse the gap between self and world? Kant replies in the affirmative. While we can never know the world-in-itself, what we can know is the world as it appears to us as human beings, with our sensory apparatus, categories of understanding, and structures of reason. From this, systematic philosophical knowledge can be constructed. Likewise, German Idealism also affirms the ability of human beings to traverse the self-world relation, because the Absolute itself traverses all beings, inclusive of human beings. Subjectivity is not something opposed to the world, but something that pervades the world, manifesting itself in its highest form in the human being. The real is rational, universal history consummates itself in human history, and the Absolute in its various guises (Spirit, Ego, Nature) pervades the entirety of reality in a continuous, quasi-vitalist flux and flow.

Once again Schopenhauer is the nay-sayer. Not only can the self-world breach not be crossed, but human beings are in no particularly unique position in regards to this. There is no conciliatory move, as we have in Kant, where human knowledge is possible but in a highly attenuated way, and there is no heroic move, as we have in thinkers like Hegel and Fichte, where the human being triumphs over the world by recognizing itself as part of the world. For Schopenhauer, the best we as human beings can do is register this limit, that the world may be acknowledged but cannot be known, that the world may make a difference in our human lives, but it remains in itself indifferent to our hopes, desires, and disappointments. In so far as the world is non-human, we who are a part of that world are also non-human. In so far as the world has *no reason* for being at all, so do we as human beings have no "sufficient reason" for existing. Let us take stock of these different positions. Can the gap between self and world be traversed? Kant: no – German Idealism: yes – Schopenhauer: no. Given this, is the human in a privileged position vis-à-vis this self-world relationship? Kant: yes – German Idealism: yes – Schopenhauer: no. As we can see, if Kant holds the middle way (no/yes), then German Idealism is on the affirmative (should we say, optimistic) side (yes/yes), while grumpy old Schopenhauer paradoxically affirms a double negative (no/no).

* * *

The Specter of Eliminativism. Such logical hair-splitting is manifest in contemporary speculative philosophy. At a recent conference given at The New School in New York, Steven Shaviro characterized contemporary speculative philosophy as polarized between the poles of "panpsychism" and "eliminativism." Such a polarization relies on a number of presuppositions. If one accepts that philosophy is broadly conditioned by the correlation between self and world (but also subject and object, or thought and the intentional object of thought), and if one accepts that this "correlationism" is a central problematic within philosophy (in so far as philosophy is by definition unable to think outside of correlationism), then for Shaviro this leaves one of two extremes open for philosophy. Either one must opt for a kind of diffuse immanence, in which some quasi-monist entity (thought, affect, object, life, etc.) is already everywhere – the view of panpsychism – or one must opt for an equally diffuse reductionism, in which all claims about existing entities are in themselves groundless, masking a potential void within everything – the view of eliminativism. In Shaviro's presentation, current speculative philosophy is being polarized between, on the one hand, a view of everything-already-everywhere, and on the other hand, a view of nothing-ultimately-nowhere.

As I read them, Shaviro's comments are meant more as a provocation than a proof. In his talk he also notes alternatives that avoid moving towards either pole: "I should also note though... that there is also the alternative of abrogating both eliminativism and panpsychism at the same time."[192] Shaviro cites the work of Reza Negarestani, Ben Woodard, and myself as examples, noting that "these thinkers have a very negative view of the efficacy of thought, and in that sense they're eliminativists. And yet they couldn't find the universe as horrible as they find it, in this Lovecraftian way, without being kinds of inverted panpsychists..."[193] However, what remains an open question is the way in which the work of Negarestani, Woodard, and myself arbitrates between eliminativism and panpsychism – whether it is in the form of a synthesis, an implosion, a double negation, or something else altogether. But it is worth noting how this alternative described by Shaviro, which would avoid both the plenum of panpsychism and the reductionism of eliminativism, results in a paradoxical plenum of nothing, or better, a notion of immanence that is indissociable from nothingness. In short, the implosion of becoming and un-becoming into Schopenhauer's "will-to-nothing" or Willlessness.

Eliminativism is more commonly understood as a branch of analytical philosophy that also goes by the name of "eliminative materialism."[194] Often associated with thinkers such as Paul Churchland and Daniel Dennett, eliminative materialism questions the existence of "qualia" such as mental states, psychological behaviors, or subjective affects. At its most extreme, it challenges any claims for an independently-existing mind beyond a neurological and biological basis. As fields such as cognitive science progress, many commonly-held notions such as "belief" or "desire" will be discovered to have no viable scientific basis and may even be relegated to the dust heap of folk psychology. Eliminativism also has a broader significance, especially in the philosophy of science, where it questions the existence of any entity beyond its material basis (be it of the vitalist "soul" or the "luminiferous ether").

Shaviro's comments are, of course, meant to evoke a different type of eliminativism, one that would take up its fundamental challenge to philosophy's principle of sufficient reason, while also departing from eliminative materialism's fidelity to biological, neurological, or physical "baseline" concepts. In a way, traditional eliminative materialism doesn't go far enough; or, put differently, given its critical questioning of basic philosophical premises, eliminative materialism's reliance on positivist science can only seem as an arbitrary stopping-point. Why claim that subjective states or psychological categories like "faith," "joy," "despondency," or "dereliction" can only be assessed to the degree that they reduce to the biological or neurological level, and then not continue on to "eliminate" that biological or neurological basis as well? It would seem that, for eliminative materialism, philosophy once again re-instates its Kantian, juridical capacity to regulate boundaries and re-establish grounds, precisely at the moment that it questions the concept of "ground" altogether. In short, this more ambiguous, "dark" eliminativism would suggest that any eliminative materialism must ultimately eliminate matter itself.[195]

The trials and tribulations (mostly tragic) of "life" as a philosophical concept readily lend themselves to the eliminativist approach. Surely no other concept has been so vociferously asserted and questioned, from historical debates over vitalism in the philosophy of science, to contemporary evocations of "vibrant matter" and "the life of things." Eliminativism haunts the ontology of life, constantly questioning its theological pretentions, while also maintaining a minimal baseline or ground that would enable fields like neuroscience to make scientifically sound claims about what is or isn't living. At its extreme, the search for a material basis for life (be it in a molecule or even, ironically, in biological "information") ends up reducing life to its material constituents – at which point there is no life at all... or there is nothing but life. Interestingly, eliminativist approaches to the ontology of life tend to split it along the lines that Shaviro describes: either everything is alive or nothing is alive; either everything is pulsating flux and flow, auto-affecting and self-transforming, or everything is silence, stillness, and the enigmatic, vacuous hum of nothingness.

For both Aristotle and Kant, the proliferating, generous, and over-present manifestations of life are always shadowed by a concept of life-in-itself that must, by necessity, enter the eliminativist abyss. Nowhere is the awareness of this duplicity more evident than in post-Kantian Idealism. In Schelling's *Naturphilosophie* and his concept of the World-Soul, in Hegel's meditations on the organicist flows of Spirit, and in Fichte's lectures on "Absolute Life," one sees in Idealism a concerted attempt to ameliorate this shadowy aspect of life itself, while also refusing the options of either mechanistic science or a return to Scholastic theology.

In contrast to this tradition, one also finds thinkers like Schopenhauer, the misanthrope from Danzig who, again and again, rails against his contemporaries for not having adequately grasped the nothingness at the heart of life itself. But if there is nothingness at the heart of life, then how does one account for its prodigious generosity and overpresence? How does one think the negation at the heart of life, when life is commonly understood to be the concept of affirmation *par excellence*? Despite the animosities between them, this is the question that concerns the Idealists as well as Schopenhauer; and it is a problem first fully articulated by Kant.

Post-Kantian Idealism did not end with Fichte, Schelling, or Hegel. In a way, its conceptual contours are resurrected by subsequent generations. A thread runs from the notion of life-as-generation to philosophical vitalism and biophilosophies inspired by

Deleuze or Bergson, just as another thread runs from the notion of life-as-givenness to the phenomenology of life, the life-world, or the flesh, as found in Husserl, Merleau-Ponty, or Michel Henry. Are we, for example, witness to a contemporary post-Kantian Idealism today, in the correlationism of a neo-Fichteanism, in the transcendental geology of a neo-Schellingianism, or in the metamorphic plasticity of neo-Hegelianism?[196]

One of Schopenhauer's most contentious propositions is that all life is dark life, and thus even contemporary scientific fields such as those that study extremophiles recapitulate, through the methods of empirical science, this shift from life-in-itself as a regional problem of epistemology to a fundamental fissure within ontology. Its limit is one that Schopenhauer characterizes as life-as-nothing, life thought in terms of negation, ultimately leading Schopenhauer from a negative ontology to something that we can only call, in somewhat technical phraseology, an *affirmative meontology* of life.

5

Last Words, Lost Words

The Relinquished Philosopher. What baffles me is how *unwise* philosophers often are – especially those philosophers most attentive to the challenges of systematic philosophy. How can one honestly undertake a project like *Being and Time*, or *Process and Reality*, or *Difference and Repetition*, or *Being and Event*, without acknowledging the placation of a *Critique of Pure Reason*, or the delusions of a *Phenomenology of Spirit*? Surely every philosopher feels, deep down, that if we could have figured it out by now, we would have done so long ago? All that has changed is that we publish more books, not better books. Perhaps this is why Heidegger, Whitehead, and others left their books unfinished, why Schopenhauer kept on adding material to *The World as Will and Representation*, why Wittgenstein retired early, and why Nietzsche and Cioran never bothered in the first place – as if they each awoke from their own dogmatic hangovers, and realized, too late, the futility of the realist impulse. Or, perhaps they understood that one begins philosophy the moment one abandons it.

* * *

A Very, Very, Very Short History of Philosophy. Philosophical realism in the West is built upon three pillars, pillars that are shaky, full of fractures, and mottled with peeling paint. The first pillar, a classical one, is that of Plato. With Plato we are introduced to a two-world view, a world of the here-and-now and a world beyond, a world that is immediately given and a world that is far off or at least inaccessible. While innumerable commentaries have been written about this or that aspect of

Plato's allegory of the cave, its basic message is quite clear – "there's got to be more." What is simply given is fine, but it's not enough, cannot be enough... no, there's got to be more. Perhaps another world lies above or beyond this one, perhaps it's co-extensive with it and we just don't realize it; but there has to be more. No doubt Plato learned this from the so-called Pre-Socratic philosophers. Air-dropped into a world one has neither created nor asked for, the self gazes about, perhaps bewildered, horrified, or fascinated, and asks the primordial philosophical question – "is this it?" Answering this question means parceling out the world that is questioned, a self that is questioning, and a problematic relation between them. As we know, for Plato this was not it, and beyond every particular chair or book or jellyfish was an abstract, perfected form of chairness, bookness, jelly-fishness. And, while Plato has been overturned many times in philosophy, the intuition of the two worlds remains, though it often goes under different names, each of which stands in for this basic relationship between the world as given and another world, perhaps more fundamental, that is not given – the One, Logos, God, noumena, the Absolute, Spirit, Will-to-Power, Being, duration, process, difference, the One...

The second pillar, a modern one, is that of Descartes. If Plato gives us the intuition of the two worlds, then Descartes gives us the means of traveling between them. Descartes' celebrated, by now cliché, phrase *Cogito ergo sum* is more than an affirmation of the self-conscious, reasoning, human subject. It is the assertion of a sufficient and necessary link between thought and the world. More specifically, it is the assertion of a consonance between human thought and the two worlds, one of which is immediately given, and the other of which is not apparent and must be mediated in some way. Descartes even goes so far as to suggest that the way to get to the world beyond is through the world here-and-now. The *Meditations* makes this clear in its narrative arc. One has simply to sit down next to a fire with a warm sweater, maybe a cup of coffee, and think. In fact, the *Meditations* is a performative text, in which Descartes-the-character shows us how to get from the world here-and-now to the world beyond. But there are many bumps along the road, and bit by bit the world here-and-now becomes more and more unreliable, more and more like a nebulous, spectral world beyond, full of anima-tronic puppets, ghosts in the machine, and trickster-demons. The secret that everyone knows about the *Meditations* is that once Descartes starts down the path of skepticism, there is no good *reason* to stop, ever. God (the philosopher's God, the God of Descartes, Leibniz, and yes, of Spinoza too) comes in to save the day, but we don't really buy it. A *deus ex machina* if ever there was one. Of course, the irony of the *Meditations* is that one has come full circle: the philosopher has traveled into the beyond in order to discover the self, the world beyond looks a lot like the world here-and-now, and one has simply arrived at where one had begun.

The third pillar is that of Kant. Admittedly, Kant is a boring writer (though better than Hegel, who is simply a bad writer). But what Kant did for philosophy is something that has had mixed blessings – he gave philosophy a job description. Certainly philosophers had had jobs prior to Kant's time, but they were either beholden to religious institutions ("you can teach Aristotle's logic, but stay away from biology," etc.) or they functioned in a transient zone prior to the disciplinary divisions of the humanities and the sciences (take Descartes – philosopher, mathematician, and amateur anatomist). Kant's critical philosophy is widely known for its delimiting effects vis-à-vis philosophy. It says what philosophy is *not*. "Yes, debate the existence of God all you like, and for as long as you like, but you will never reach a philosophically adequate answer, and philoso-phers shouldn't be bothering with this anyways – that is the job of the priests." It is also a sobering up for philosophy as a privi-leged, human endeavor; it says what philosophy cannot do –

notably, it cannot ever fully bridge the gap between the domain of phenomena (the world as it appears to us) and noumena (the world in itself, apart from our experience of it). Kant's critical philosophy is remarkable because it harbors within itself a contradiction – it is a grand, shimmering, systematic philosophy, a sort of cathedral of philosophy – that argues for philosophy's humility... even for philosophy's poverty.

But even Kant's conciliatory gesture has a happy ending, for while we may not know the world in itself, we can know how we know, and we can study how the world appears to us, and maybe – just maybe – by doing this we can at least minimally infer that there is "something more" out there, making an impression on us, in whatever inevitably distorted way we may intuit it.

From a certain vantage point, the history of Western philosophy looks like a somewhat panicky, feverish attempt to cover up the suspicion that there may not be more. Every excited, anxious assertion of "there's got to be more" covers up a more disappointing, more morose, "this is it."

All of this leaves out a possible fourth pillar – that of Nietzsche – who excitedly asserts "this is it!" And so realism returns to its pessimistic roots.

* * *

Phantasms (I). "All that is visible rests upon the invisible – the audible upon the inaudible – the felt upon the unfelt. Perhaps thinking rests upon unthinking."[197]

* * *

Here... Everything is by Design. In the history of philosophy, there is no single, agreed-upon definition of "realism." Depending on what one thinks about philosophy, this is an occasion for concern or for laughter. And yet nearly every philosophy relies on some realist claim, a claim to be able to finally and definitively articulate "the way things are" – no matter how strange or counter-intuitive such claims may seem. In fact, it could be argued that the criteria of realism in philosophy today is precisely how counter-intuitive and "weird" the claims are for the real. But inevitably disagreements arise, schools are formed, weighty academic tomes are published, and academic tribalism abounds.

In many philosophies, what is at stake is a claim about the real, though no two claims are alike. Historians of philosophy usually resolve this by simply enumerating the realisms promoted by various philosophers, one following the next in a neat, sequential progression: Platonic realism (the world I see before me and the world of abstract forms), Aristotelian realism (the abstract forms as inseparable from the world I see before me), Hegelian realism (the world in itself as commensurate with the structure of thought), Whiteheadian realism (process, becoming, and change as primary; substances, objects, and things as secondary), and so on. Another approach is to brand the types of realism in a trans-historical manner, as they cross historical epochs and individual thinkers: a naïve realism (in which appearance and reality are the same), an epistemological realism (reality is distinct from appearance, and reality resides in abstract universals; philosophy's goal is to interrogate not appearances but the universals), and an ontological realism (that which exists is real, even if not actual).

But in such lists and tables we are obliged to mention another kind of realism, for which we must thank Kant, and which he would undoubtedly call a critical realism – a realism that doesn't presume that the real – whether tangible or not – can be adequately known. It is almost an agnostic realism, though in saying this we have already begun, according to Kant, to depart from the domain of philosophy proper. Kant brings us the most modern realism that is at the same time indelibly premodern (dare we say, mystical).

* * *

What You See Is What You Get. Simplifying to the extreme, we might offer the following: philosophical realism is predicated on two related but distinct approaches. The first is the "what you see is what you get" approach, the attempt to understand something without subjective bias, without idealism, without distortion. The second is the "just the facts" approach, or the attempt to understand something as it is without reliance on speculation, hypotheses, guesswork, or hoping for the best. In a way, the second approach follows from the first. In the first, what appears to be a value-neutral acceptance of the "way things are" relies to a great degree on the experience of a cognizing subject – and subjective experience is, as we know, not the most reliable of measures for realism. "What you see is what you get," yes, but what I get is not necessarily what you get, and vice-versa. One then moves to the second approach, attempting, as it were, to by-pass the perennially problematic area of experience, while not totally jettisoning the domain of empirical sense data. What is real is what can be verified, measured, analyzed, articulated as an object of study. One parses out experience into an elaborate architectonics of cognitive functions (sensibility, understanding, reason), or one "brackets" the world in its appearing to us as an object of study, or one prioritizes becoming over being, the continuous over the discrete, process over product, or one makes a turn away from reality in itself towards language, logic, and signs, or one enlists the descriptive rigor of mathematical set theory and its capacity for managing parts and the whole. The approaches vary, but the upshot is that what is real is indisputable, apart from our desires, hopes, and wish-fulfillments. But this too runs into problems, in that someone is always doing the measuring, a decision has been made about the sort of logical game we will play today, and the criteria for verification are at best moving targets. The apotheosis of this "scientific" realism is tautology – the real is... real. Besides, one person's reality is another's fantasy, regardless of – or indeed because of – how finely it is measured.

* * *

What to Do With Thought. There is a pessimism that is built into all attempts at a philosophy of realism. Philosophy's desperate push to attain the real is matched only its inability to do so. Realizing this, one rescinds realism, but not reason. A new problem arises, a problem specific to pessimism – what then to do with thought.

* * *

Phantasms (II). A realist claim is not always a claim about the real, just as all claims about the real are realist – but not necessarily realistic.

* * *

Depressive Realism. Pessimism and realism seem to be two very different ways of thinking. Realism implies a certain neutrality, seeing things the way they are, apart from self-interest or the interest of others, a neutralization of value that always seems to end in the vaguely streetwise tautology of "it is what it is." Pessimism, by contrast, is often regarded as a bad attitude more than a philosophical position. It is always opposed to optimism, if not logically then affectively. If pessimists are enthusiastic about anything, it is about *pessimus*, "the worst," resplendent in every possible outcome, glimmering around every corner, an *ecstasy of the worst* that is shrouded by a grimace or curmudgeonly grunt. Realism is often employed by necessity – one is never a realist "just for fun." As a philosophical position, the necessity of realism is usually elicited by something non-philosophical – politics, science, or just getting things done. Pessimism is a luxury – one must have spare time to complain, to moan and groan and write lyrical poetry about suffering – all of which helps no one and in fact makes things worse.

That said, there is a connection between pessimism and realism. One example comes not from philosophy but from psychology. "Depressive realism" is the official-sounding name that has been given to the proposition that a pessimistic outlook gives one a "healthier" and more realistic grasp of one's life and the world in which one lives. The pessimist – so the argument goes – is freed from the "locus of control" fallacy; they do not believe that they are in total control of their actions and their destiny. Pessimists are also less likely to presume that bad things always happen to other people (the "optimism bias"), and as a result, the pessimist holds no illusions about their own superiority over other people. They hold no high hopes, great expectations, or illusions of grandeur. They live and act, for now, for the time being, and if things don't work out, well, what did you expect?

The jury still seems to be out on whether this is a viable psychological theory or simply an attempt to view depression optimistically. Contemporary philosophers seem to have caught the bug, putting out pop-philosophy books that, in their almost absurd earnestness, begin to sound like self-help. However, at the broadest level – one that exceeds psychology – might we add that the pessimist holds no illusions, not just about one's own individual being, but about the superiority or relevance of all human beings? Indeed, of all beings – of Being? If this is a realism, then it is a realism that extends into antihumanism – a sort of species-wide depression.

* * *

Born in the Ruins of Philosophy. At any given moment in time, the pillars of philosophy are nearly indistinguishable from ruins. They may still stand, but they serve less an architectural function and are more like tourist attractions. As ruins, they are filled with cracks and fissures, but no one really is to blame, except of course the philosophers. And the demolition of philosophy is always carried out by philosophy itself (for who else cares enough to so thoroughly examine every niche of the ruins in order to spackle them over?). Historians of philosophy are the clean-up crew. In the meantime, those loiterers known as antiphilosophers keep hanging around, sometimes hidden in their nearby caves, sometimes just sitting about like lumps of syllogistic clay. They are those who are skeptics, cynics, nihilists, pessimists. They refuse to live within the ruins, in the shadow of the pillars, but they also haven't left the site for better weather or tolerable coffee. The way they think sounds philosophical – skeptic*ism*, nihil*ism*, pessim*ism* – terms that seem to denote methods, schools, traditions. But they also know that everything built up must collapse again, and this intuition is evident within their very words – the all-too-convincing self-doubt of Pascal, the funereal spite of Schopenhauer, the stark transmissions of Cioran...

But there is still a philosophical question embedded in their aphorisms, fragments, and missives against humanity. With skepticism, one must always answer the question, "where does doubt stop?" Every philosopher finds their own stopping point: doubt stops at God, doubt stops at self-consciousness, doubt stops at logical consistency, and so on. Of course, for some, doubt doesn't stop, and so the skeptic overlaps with the nihilist. With pessimism, the question is different: how many "no"s make a "yes"? Every philosopher negates something in the world or about the world – a presumption, an article of faith, what passes as common sense. But this negation always paves the way for a further affirmation, a claim about how things really are. As with skepticism, there is also the possibility of a "no" that never leads to a "yes," a "no" that must, as a consequence, devolve upon and devour itself, leading to paradox and contradiction. The outcome is suicide (the modern version), self-abnegation (the mystical, premodern version), or tragedy (the classical version). We've forgotten the postmodern version – farce, slapstick, gallows humor.

* * *

Variations on Misanthropy (Brassier). Billions of years from now, the sun will die. Our planet may very well die before that, or at least become inhospitable for carbon-based life forms. Species on the planet become extinct at a "natural background rate" of one to five species per year, though figures for our current era are upwards of ten thousand times that rate. The current global human population is 7 billion, though health officials tell us the planet can sustain a population of 1.5 billion. The average global human life expectancy is 73 years for women, 68 years for men. The chance that a person will have a life-threatening condition or disease is upwards of 30-40%, even in developed countries.[198]

At what point do you become concerned? Implicitly or explicitly, this is a question that confronts every person. Most likely, any concerns we have about the death of the sun billions of years from now are trumped by our more immediate concerns over the next flu season. In addition, all these figures are tied to each other. The rate of the extinction of species has exponentially increased alongside the exponential increase in the human population. Human beings take up 42% of the planet's total terrestrial net primary productivity, 30% of its total marine productivity, 40% of the planet's land is used for human food production, and 50% of the planet's total land mass has been transformed for human use.[199]

And yet, there is a certain inevitability in the sun's death, just as there is in our own deaths. This inevitability is matched by its being a limit for thought. As individuals, something survives our own death. We are remembered or memorialized (or, perhaps, cursed) by others who survive us, and, even though the individual person dies, the species continues. But, in the case of human extinction, who will give testimony to this, who will experience it, who will be there to apprehend and comprehend it? In so far as we human beings have raised ourselves above all other species largely by virtue of our consciousness and cognition – our ability to be aware of our being alive, of our being thinking beings, of our existence as such – then the extinction of humanity presents a conundrum, encapsulated by Ray Brassier: "How does thought think a world without thought? Or more urgently: How does thought think the death of thinking?"[200]

Extinction is more than a thought problem, but a problem for thought itself. It is as much a scientific problem as it is an existential one. And the extinction of the human species – a biological inevitability – is abetted by other kinds of extinction, the extinction of all life resulting from the sun's death, the extinction of all matter from the universe's continual gravitational expansion.

Of course, I as a human subject will not be around to experience those extinctions (except perhaps in a movie), existing as they do on the scale of billions and trillions of years. And yet, even the furthest extinction described to us by science haunts us with a secret message: *"Everything is dead already."*[201] Against the romantic reveries of an unbounded future of human possibility and potential, the sciences of cosmology, astrophysics, geology, and population biology reveal to us a finitude that is, ultimately, a philosophical finitude: "The extinction of the sun is a catastrophe, a mis-turning or over-turning (*kata-strophe*) because it blots out the terrestrial horizon of future possibility relative to which human existence, and hence philosophical questioning, have hitherto oriented themselves."[202] Thought, the very thing by which we as human beings have elevated ourselves into a future of infinite possibility, is also that which undermines that very act of self-elevation. The culmination of thought is, in a way, to bring down that which it has raised up; thought fulfilled in its own negation. Brassier again: "...extinction indexes the thought of the absence of thought."[203]

That this is gained through the results of scientific inquiry is significant. Extinction – and the enigmatic thought of extinction – is a product of the legacy of the Enlightenment, with human reason and human self-reliance at the center of its ideology. But Enlightenment is also Janus-faced; it decenters in order to re-center. It displaces the earth from the center of the universe, in order to place human scientific reason back in the center. "The earth is not the center, but at least we know this." One result of this decentering and recentering is an increasing difference between the world as we experience it phenomenally and the world described to us by the increasingly specialized and counter-intuitive sciences.[204]

Furthermore, extinction – as a scientific description of an external finitude or limit to thought – renders thought as more than a subjective interiority, more than an intentional consciousness that selectively interfaces with the outside world. Extinction forces thought to be externalized: "Extinction turns thinking inside out, objectifying it as a perishable thing in the world like any other."[205] Extinction subsumes everything within its ambit, even the self-valorizing transcendence of human thought, with its critical distance and intellectual intuitions.

Far from advocating the dream of infinite human potential, Enlightenment becomes something different in the case of extinction. It is no longer reason in the service of human well-being. Rather, Enlightenment becomes "an unavoidable corollary of the realist conviction that there is a mind-independent reality, which, despite the presumptions of human narcissism, is indifferent to our existence and oblivious to the 'values' and 'meanings' which we would drape over it in order to make it more hospitable."[206] In a sense, the Enlightenment has worked too well; human beings are the problem, not the solution: "the disenchantment of the world understood as a consequence of the process whereby the Enlightenment shattered the 'great chain of being' and defaced the 'book of the world' is a necessary consequence of the coruscating potency of reason, and hence an invigorating vector of intellectual discovery, rather than a calamitous diminishment."[207]

However, the Enlightenment not only counters the previously dominant model of theology and religion (a disenchantment of an enchantment), but Enlightenment science also produces its own enchantment (or re-enchantment) through the language of science rather than religion. The wonders of nature explained by science, the diversity of catalogued flora and fauna, and mysteries of the mind and body mechanically revealed, all point to this Janus-faced decentering and recentering of the human.

The sun will die, species go extinct, human life extends. But who ever said that reason – much less thought – was exclusively human? If followed to its conclusion, this affirmative Enlightenment of enchantment leads to a negative Enlightenment of disenchantment. The enchantment of nature, life, and the cosmos engendered by the sciences also has a dark side, a "disenchantment of the world" that reduces human self-valorization (inclusive of the totalizing pretentions of the sciences) to an act of self-nullification. If Brassier is a thinker of the Enlightenment, it is of this type of negative Enlightenment, one for which the extinction of all thought becomes the starting point for a philosophy, not its end: "Thinking has interests that do not coincide with those of living; indeed, they can have been pitted against the latter."[208] Perhaps, contra Descartes, we should not say "I think," but rather, "I am thought."

* * *

Towards a Philosophy of Futility. While it often has a quasi-philosophical status, pessimism is ultimately dismissed because it commits that most unforgiveable of philosophical errors – it mistakes the subjective for the objective. But the acknowledgement of this error is already embedded within pessimism. This is the reason why Schopenhauer's *The World as Will and Representation* only looks like a work of systematic philosophy. Really, by the book's final sections, the "whole" has given way to crumbling, grumbling ruins and furtive appeals to quasi-Buddhist "nothingness." He should've known better. Nevertheless, every pessimistic thinker understands at some level the pessimism inherent in the philosophical enterprise. The challenge of any philosophy is to account for its own horizon, its own limits, what it cannot say, know, or think.

This is why there is no "analytical pessimism" in philosophy, only a metaphysical poetics of finitude and angst. No one has ever claimed a scientific status for pessimism. That is, almost no one. An exception is the late 19th century American author Edgar Saltus, who, near the end of his book *The Philosophy of Disenchantment* is curiously optimistic about what he calls a "scientific pessimism" of the future. But Saltus' scientific pessimism is as much about a mystical revelation of limits as it is about logical rigor and verifiable claims. Science in the service of pessimism, it seems.

Eduard von Hartmann, discipline of Schopenhauer, takes a different route. In his massive, unwieldy *The Philosophy of the Unconscious*, Hartmann attempts to wed Schopenhauer's pessimism with the biology and physics of his day. The entirety of the first part of his work contains detailed descriptions of scientific experiments involving the decapitation of animals – as if to suggest a stark allegory between science and philosophy. But all that science teaches Hartmann is that the human species is at best an accident that has had the misfortune of thinking itself a necessity. As accidentally as we have come into being, so must we accidentally move out of being.

Then there is Nietzsche, the defiant convalescent, who rails as much against science as he does religion, telling us that we have not gone far enough in our pessimism, not yet attained a "pessimism of strength." And yet, as he jibes, what we need now is "a chemistry of the moral, religious, aesthetic representations and sensations, likewise of all those stimuli that we experience within ourselves amid the wholesale and retail transactions of culture and society, indeed even in solitude." But that is not all. Given this, Nietzsche asks, "what if this chemistry were to reach the conclusion that in this area too, the most magnificent colors have been extracted from base, even despised materials?"[209]

All of this would seem to require a distinct branch of philosophy dedicated to studying the futility of all attempts to philosophize. Perhaps pessimism has a future after all. One imagines massive tomes of systematic philosophy with self-contradictory titles such as *The Philosophy of Futility*. But the thing is that such a proposition is ultimately, for the pessimist, tedious and pedantic. As a philosophy, pessimism is always half-hearted, ready to give up or abandon a line of thought at the slightest inclination. Pessimism – speaking (as it feels obliged to do) in its deep, resounding, philosophical tones – says that all philosophies must fail, no matter what methods they deploy or from which tradition they may stem. All philosophies must fail because their truth claims must by necessity be partial, contingent, and grounded in some basis that cannot itself be directly questioned; its claims are contingent because its authority relies on propositions, those peculiar, hallucinatory uses of a language of effective rigor. Propositions in language, with the aid of bounded concepts, through the structure of logical argumentation, all framed by the basic relation of intentionality and the self-world relation. The result is that pessimism is often relegated to the dungeons or the attics of philosophy. It is forced to witness or to wait for its own failure, in a series of infinite resignations: No philosophy can say anything about everything... no philosophy can say everything about anything...

* * *

Pascal's Abyss. In one of his notebooks Pascal comments on a central paradox concerning humanity's ceaseless quest for knowledge: the more we learn, the more we learn how insignificant we are. Whether our knowledge is true or false matters little, for if our knowledge is false, "then there is no truth in man," and if our knowledge is true, then humanity "has good cause to feel humiliated."[210] For Pascal, this disproportion of humanity strikes him as cause for a species-level humility, even shame.

One need not be a scientist or a philosopher to do this. Let any person contemplate, even for a moment, the known universe, radiating outwards from our dark, blinding sun:

> ...let him see the earth as a mere speck compared to the vast orbit described by this star, and let him marvel at finding this vast orbit itself to be no more than the tiniest point compared to that described by the stars revolving in the firmament. But if our eyes stop there, let our imagination proceed further; it will grow weary of conceiving things before nature tires of producing them... The whole visible world is only an imperceptible dot... we only bring forth atoms compared to the reality of things.[211]

Things don't stop there. What follows for the macrocosm also follows for the microcosm:

> I want to show him a new abyss. I want to depict to him not

only the visible universe, but all the conceivable immensity of nature enclosed in this miniature atom. Let him see there an infinity of universes, each with its firmament, its planets, its earth, in the same proportions as in the visible world, and on that earth animals, and finally mites, in which he will find again the same results as the first; and finding the same thing yet again in the others without end or respite, he will be lost in such wonders, as astounding in the minuteness as the others in their amplitude.[212]

Such terrifying reveries – now the stock-and-trade of any educational program on cosmology – lead Pascal to a formulation for which we is now well-known: "Nature is an infinite sphere whose center is everywhere and circumference nowhere."[213]

What Pascal discovers here is a thought of total uncertainty, achieved by a simple shift of scale – above the human, and below the human. As creatures of a highly limited granularity, we as human beings tend to view the world almost exclusively on our own level. Hence the world is the world-for-us, there for our taking, designed for our various interventions and designs, and in our tenuous moments of scientific euphoria, if we dare to posit a world-in-itself independent of human observers, it is only to further bolster our deeply engrained faith in the world-for-us.

This troubles Pascal. And, in this particular fragment, Pascal the geometer is quickly followed by Pascal the theologian. In the very next line he writes: "In short it is the greatest perceptible mark of God's omnipotence that our imagination should lose itself in that thought."[214] And so order on the human scale is superseded by order on the cosmic scale, and our inability to comprehend this cosmos is itself superseded by our recognition of this thought collapsing in on itself – a collapsing that is, for Pascal, the mark of the divine.

I find Pascal's repeated turns to religious faith disappointing, especially because they always seem to occur just at the moment where he has revealed the limitations of the human, only to be saved, at the last moment, by mathematics or mysticism. But I am, for a second, consoled in this particular fragment of Pascal's, for his ecstatic musings take yet another turn:

> Let man, returning to himself, consider what he is in comparison with what exists; let him regard himself as lost, and from this little dungeon, in which he finds himself lodged, I mean the universe, let him learn to take the earth, its realms, its cities, its houses and himself at their proper value.[215]

Pascal seems to have been vindicated by modern cosmology. Scientists tell us that, "roughly" one trillion, trillion, trillion years from now, the ever-expanding universe will have reached a point at which matter itself – and the very possibility of material existence – will be obliterated. Ray Brassier summarizes their findings:

> Every star in the universe will have burnt out, plunging the cosmos into a state of absolute darkness and leaving behind nothing but spent husks of collapsed matter. All free matter, whether on planetary surfaces or in interstellar space, will have decayed, eradicating any remnants of life based in protons and chemistry, and erasing every vestige of sentience – irrespective of its physical basis. Finally, in a state cosmologists call "asymptopia," the stellar corpses littering the empty universe will evaporate into a brief hailstorm of elementary particles. Atoms themselves will cease to exist. Only the implacable gravitational expansion will continue, driven by the current inexplicable force called "dark energy," which will keep pushing the extinguished universe deeper and deeper into an eternal and unfathomable blackness.[216]

And so the human being discovers, at last, that its existence has always been subtended by its non-existence, that it dies the moment it lives, and that, perhaps, we do nothing but carry around a corpse that itself carries around the sullen grey matter that occasionally wonders if the same sullen stars that occupy every firmament at every scale also occupy this starry speculative corpse.

Notes

Portions of this book have previously appeared in the following publications: *Mute; Parrhesia; Postmedieval; Radical Philosophy; Realism, Materialism, Art* (eds. Christopher Cox and Suhail Malik); *Speculative Medievalisms* (eds. Eileen Joy et al.); and at lectures given at the Kings College Anatomy Theatre (London), the Natural History Museum (London), the University of California Berkeley, the University of Chicago. My gratitude to those involved in organizing these publications and events. Special thanks to the crew at Zero Books. Thanks also to AR, AS, ELT, JA, MST, MT, NM, RB, SC, TG, TL, and PM.

1. René Descartes, *Meditations and Other Metaphysical Writings*, trans. Desmond Clarke (New York: Penguin, 1998), p. 18.
2. Ibid.
3. Ibid., p. 22.
4. Ibid., p. 24.
5. Ibid.
6. Thomas De Quincey, "The Last Days of Immanuel Kant," in *The Last Days of Immanuel Kant and Other Writings – De Quincey's Works, Volume III* (Edinburgh: Adam and Charles Black, 1871), p. 164. De Quincey – author, opium addict, and friend of the Lake Poets – bases his account on that of Ehregott Andreas Wasianski, pastor and friend of Kant.
7. Ibid., p. 165.
8. Ibid.
9. E.M. Cioran, *A Short History of Decay*, trans. Richard Howard (New York: Arcade, 2012), p. 47.
10. Immanuel Kant, "On the Power of the Mind to Master Its Morbid Feelings by Sheer Resolution," in *The Conflict of the Faculties*, in *Religion and Rational Theology*, ed. and trans. Allan W. Wood and George Di Giovanni (Cambridge:

Cambridge University Press, 2001), p. 318. As per the convention of his time, Kant doesn't use the term "depression" but either "melancholia" or "hypochrondria."

11. Ibid.
12. Ibid.
13. Kant, *Critique of Judgement*, trans. James Creed Meredith (Oxford: Clarendon, 1957), p. 129, "General Remark on the Exposition of Aesthetic Reflective Judgements."
14. Ibid., p. 317.
15. Ibid.
16. See Kant, "An attempt at some reflections on optimism...", in *Theoretical Philosophy, 1755-1770*, ed. and trans. David Walford with Ralf Meerbote (Cambridge: Cambridge University Press, 2003).
17. Kant, "The End of All Things," in *Religion and Rational Theology*, p. 224.
18. De Quincey, "The Last Days of Immanuel Kant," p. 163.
19. According to Wasianski's account, the words "it is enough" (*es ist genug*) had a more humble origin: they were a reply to Wasianski giving the ailing, weak Kant a drink of water. And so a different kind of profundity emerges, a more tragic-comic one.
20. Friedrich Nietzsche, "On Truth and Lie in an Extra-Moral Sense," in *The Portable Nietzsche*, ed. and trans. Walter Kaufmann (New York: Viking, 1964), p. 42.
21. As a book, *Human, All Too Human* is often under-represented in Nietzsche scholarship. *Beyond Good and Evil* and *The Genealogy of Morals* are frequently taught in the classroom, *Thus Spoke Zarathustra* frequently cited for its literary merits, and late works such as *The Antichrist* and *Ecce Homo* read for their iconoclasm. A close look at *Human, All Too Human* not only shows that many of Nietzsche's later concepts were already present there in nascent form, but it also brings much of the later work back into the broader issue of the

problem of the human being. Many claims have been made for Nietzsche by later generations – a nihilist Nietzsche, an existential Nietzsche, a political Nietzsche, a feminist Nietzsche, a quantum Nietzsche, even a cyber-Nietzsche. A proposition, then: If there is a Nietzsche for our twenty-first century of planetary disaster, extinction, and the "posthuman," it resides not in his later work, but in the two volumes of *Human, All Too Human*.

22. Friedrich Nietzsche, *Human, All Too Human II and Unpublished Fragments from the Period of Human, All Too Human II (Spring 1878-Fall 1879)*, trans. Gary Handwerk (Stanford: Stanford University Press, 2013), pp. 158-59.

23. Ibid., p. 159.

24. In *Ecce Homo* Nietzsche recounts how, upon the publication of *Human, All Too Human*, he had sent two copies to Wagner, from whom he had definitively separated. By coincidence, Wagner had at the same time sent him a copy of *Parsifal*. Nietzsche describes the coincidence as a moment of dissonance, "as if two swords had crossed."

25. The phrase is also an homage to Noël Carroll's book *The Philosophy of Horror; or, Paradoxes of the Heart* (New York: Routledge, 1990), which manages to find a balance between analytical explication and philosophical openness.

26. Georges Bataille, *Guilty*, trans. Bruce Boone (Venice, CA: Lapis Press, 1988), p. 12.

27. Pseudo-Dionysius, *The Mystical Theology*, in *The Complete Works*, trans. Paul Rorem (New York: Paulist, 1988), p. 135.

28. Ibid., p. 136.

29. Ibid., p. 135.

30. Ibid., p. 139.

31. Vladimir Lossky, *The Mystical Theology of the Eastern Church*, trans. Fellowship of St. Alban and St. Sergius (London: James Clarke & Co., 1957), p. 28.

32. Meister Eckhart, *Sermon 4*, in *The Complete Mystical Works of*

Meister Eckhart, trans. Maurice O'C. Walshe (New York: Crossroads, 2010), p. 56.

33. Ibid.

34. Ibid., *Sermon 51*, p. 273.

35. For an overview on the role of woman in medieval Christian mysticism, see Bernard McGinn, *The Flowering of Mysticism: Men and Women in the New Mysticism, 1200-1350* (New York: Crossroad, 1998), the collection *Medieval Writings on Female Spirituality*, ed. Elizabeth Spearing (New York: Penguin, 2002), and Caroline Walker Bynum, *Holy Feast and Holy Fast* (Berkeley: University of California Press, 1988). For a consideration of the links between medieval mysticism and postmodern theory, see Amy Hollywood, *Sensible Ecstasy* (Chicago: University of Chicago Press, 2002), where Hollywood discusses, among other things, the relationship between Angela of Foligno and Georges Bataille.

36. Angela had actually outlined thirty stages of her mystical itinerary, though it appears that Brother Arnaldo, unable to make sense of the final stages, attempted to condense them into the seven supplementary stages.

37. Angela of Foligno, *The Memorial*, in *Complete Works*, trans. Paul Lachance (New York: Paulist, 1993), p. 128.

38. Ibid., p. 176.

39. Ibid., p. 182.

40. Ibid., p. 198.

41. Ibid., p. 202.

42. Ibid., p. 205.

43. *The Cloud of Unknowing*, ed. James Walsh (New York: Paulist, 1981), p. 128.

44. Ibid., p. 120.

45. Ibid., p. 128.

46. Ibid., p. 130.

47. John of the Cross, *The Dark Night of the Soul*, Book I, ch. 8.

48. Ibid., Book I, ch. 12.

49. Ibid., Book II, ch. 5.
50. Bataille, *Inner Experience*, trans. Leslie Anne Boldt (Albany: SUNY Press, 1988), pp. 4-5.
51. Bataille, *The Accursed Share*, trans. Robert Hurley (New York: Zone, 1991), p. 21.
52. Bataille, *L'Archangélique et autre poèmes* (Paris: Gallimard, 2008), pp. 32-33, translation mine. The key passage reads: *"l'excès de ténèbres / est l'éclat de l'étoile / le froid de la tombe est un dé."*
53. Bataille, *The Tears of Eros*, trans. Peter Connor (San Francisco: City Lights, 1991), pp. 206-207.
54. *Inner Experience*, p. 17.
55. Ibid., p. 33.
56. Maurice Blanchot, "The Outside, the Night," in *The Space of Literature*, trans. Ann Smock (Lincoln: University of Nebraska Press, 1982), p. 163.
57. Novalis, *Hymns to the Night*, trans. Dick Higgins (New York: McPherson & Co., 1988), p. 11.
58. Blanchot, "The Outside, the Night," p. 163.
59. Ibid.
60. Maurice Blanchot, *Thomas the Obscure*, trans. Robert Lamberton (Barrytown: Station Hill, 1988), p. 14.
61. Ibid., p. 168.
62. Ibid., p. 169.
63. Rasu-Yong Tugen, *Songs from the Black Moon* (n.p.: gnOme books, 2014), p. 58.
64. Pseudo-Leopardi, *Cantos for the Crestfallen* (n.p.: gnOme books, 2014), XXVIII.
65. Blanchot, "The Outside, the Night," p. 169.
66. Robert Fludd, *The Technical, Physical and Metaphysical History of the Macrocosm and Microcosm*, in *Robert Fludd (Western Esoteric Masters Series)*, ed. William Huffman (Berkeley: North Atlantic Books, 2001), pp. 74; 62.
67. Cited in Nicola Masciandaro, "Paradisical Pessimism: On

the Crucifixion Darkness and the Cosmic Materiality of Sorrow," manuscript, p. 6. The essay is from Masciandaro's forthcoming book *The Sorrow of Being*. The Gospel passages are from *Luke* 23:43-44 and *Matthew* 27:45-46, respectively.

68. Ibid., p. 7.

69. Ibid., p. 10.

70. Ibid., p. 11.

71. Nicola Masciandaro, "Secret: No Light Has Ever Seen the Black Universe," in Alexander Galloway, Daniel Colucciello Barber, Nicolas Masciandaro, and Eugene Thacker, *Dark Nights of the Universe* (Miami: [name], 2013), p. 60-61. This book collects talks given at an event co-sponsored by The Public School New York and Recess Gallery. The talks were structured around a short text by French philosopher François Laruelle, "Du noir univers." For more info see: http://www.recessart.org/activities/5136.

72. François Laruelle, "On the Black Universe in the Human Foundations of Color," trans. Miguel Abreu, in *Dark Nights of the Universe*, p. 106.

73. Masciandaro, "Secret," p. 61.

74. For instance, in some sections Goethe separates his discussion of "physiological" colors from "physical" and "chemical" colors. It is only after laying this groundwork that he then goes on to consider the "effect of color with reference to moral association" (i.e. in myth, religion, art, and culture).

75. Johann Wolfgang von Goethe, *Theory of Colors*, trans. Charles Lock Eastlake (Cambridge: MIT Press, 1970), p. 2.

76. The most well-known debate of this type prior to Schopenhauer was that of John Locke, who argued for a distinction between primary qualities and secondary qualities, the former being those properties that exist independent of a viewer, and the latter being those produced exclusively within the viewer. Locke considered

color to be a secondary quality, while Goethe, drawing upon the optics research of his day, suggests that color is in effect a primary quality.

77. Arthur Schopenhauer, *On Vision and Colors*, in *On Vision and Colors by Arthur Schopenhauer and Color Sphere by Philipp Otto Runge*, trans. Georg Stahl (New York: Princeton Architectural Press, 2010), p. 61.

78. If the visible spectrum has black and white at either pole, then color is some mixture or "fraction" in between. As Schopenhauer notes: "Black and white are not colors in the true sense... because they do not represent fractions, and thus no qualitative division of the retina" (p. 70).

79. Summarizing the polarized nature of the visible spectrum between white and black, Schopenhauer comments: "We have found that, by the qualitatively divided activity of the retina, the appearance of one half is essentially conditioned by the *inactivity* of the other half, at any rate at the same spot. *Inactivity* of the retina is... *total darkness*" (p. 73).

80. In the late 1940s De Kooning produced several "black drawings," though these were really expressionist white on a black background. In the 1950s Ellsworth Kelly produced his own, ultra-flat black paintings in a series of large canvases, including "Black" (1951), and later in the decade Robert Motherwell produced almost all-black canvases of his giant brush strokes (such as "Iberia no. 18," from 1958). Also in the late 50s, Robert Rauschenberg produced a thick, textual canvas of black goop, though the thickness of the paint produced a glossy, reflective surface. And throughout the 1960s several artists produced black paintings with differing degrees of hue and texture, such as in Frank Stella's geometric paintings of think white lines on near-black backgrounds. An overview is given in Stephanie Rosenthal, *Black Paintings: Robert Rauschenberg, Ad Reinhardt, Mark Rothko, Frank Stella* (Ostfildern: Hatje Cantz,

2007).

81. Laruelle, "On the Black Universe," p. 104.

82. Ibid., p. 105.

83. Ibid., p. 105-106. Laruelle continues: "As opposed to the black objectified in the spectrum, Black is already manifested, before any process of manifestation."

84. Aristotle's analysis on the topic is in *Physics* IV.6-9.

85. Aristotle, *Physics*, trans. R.P. Hardie and R.K. Gaye, in *The Complete Works of Aristotle*, ed. Jonathan Barnes (Princeton: Princeton University Press, 1991), IV.8.216a22-23, p. 367.

86. Martin Heidegger, *Being and Time*, trans. John Macquarrie and Edward Robinson (New York: HarperCollins, 1962), §2, p. 25-26, italics removed.

87. Heidegger, "What is Metaphysics?", trans. David Farrell Krell, in *Basic Writings* (New York: HarperCollins, 1977), p. 96.

88. Ibid., p. 108.

89. *Being and Time*, §62, p. 356, italics removed.

90. Jean-Paul Sartre, *Being and Nothingness*, trans. Hazel E. Barnes (New York: Washington Square Press, 1984), p. 36.

91. Ibid.

92. Ibid., p. 42. I should note that Prema's hair is dark, but not so dark that her actual presence in the café would create the illusion of dark matter, thereby effectuating another type of nothingness that is asserted as a presence (as opposed to a nothingness asserted as an absence).

93. Ibid., p. 49.

94. Alain Badiou, *Being and Event*, trans. Oliver Feltham (New York: Continuum, 2005), p. 56.

95. Sartre, *Being and Nothingness*, p. 49.

96. On Eckhart's concept of nothing/nothingness with respect to continental philosophy, see John Caputo, *The Mystical Element in Heidegger's Thought* (New York: Fordham University Press, 1986), Beverly Lanzetta, "Three Categories

of Nothingness in Eckhart," *Journal of Religion* 72.2 (1992): 248-68, and Reiner Schürmann, *Meister Eckhart, Mystic and Philosopher* (Bloomington: Indiana University Press, 1978). On Eckhart's relation to Buddhism, see Shizuteru Ueda, "Nothingness in Meister Eckhart and Zen Buddhism," in *The Buddha Eye: An Anthology of the Kyoto School and Its Contemporaries*, ed. Frederick Franck, (Bloomington: World Wisdom, 2004), pp. 157-70.

97. Meister Eckhart, *Sermon 19*, in *The Complete Mystical Works of Meister Eckhart*, p. 137.

98. Ibid., p. 140.

99. Ibid., p. 141.

100. Ibid.

101. Ibid.

102. In this way mysticism can be viewed from the viewpoint of mediation, and the mystical encounter can be regarded as an instance of "media" in a premodern sense, tipping either towards pure continuity ("immediation") or pure inaccessibility ("antimediation"). For more, see my chapter in *Excommunication: Three Inquiries in Media and Mediation*, co-authored with Alexander Galloway and McKenzie Wark (Chicago: University of Chicago Press, 2013), pp. 77ff.

103. Eckhart, *Sermon Ninety-Seven*, in *The Complete Mystical Works of Meister Eckhart*, p. 469.

104. Eckhart, *Sermon Ninety-Six*, in *The Complete Mystical Works of Meister Eckhart*, p. 465.

105. John Caputo notes this apparent duplicity in his comparison of Eckhart and the later Heidegger in his study *The Mystical Element in Heidegger's Thought* (New York: Fordham University Press, 1986).

106. Bernard McGinn, *The Mystical Thought of Meister Eckhart* (New York: Crossroad Publishing, 2001), p. 105.

107. On Eckhart's metaphysics of flow, see McGinn, *The Mystical Thought of Meister Eckhart*, pp. 72ff. As McGinn notes, God

in Eckhart is at once *bullitio* (overflowing, beneficent, generosity) and *ebullitio* (flowing onward and outward into creatures and the world).

108. This is a coinage of François Laruelle to describe the pre-philosophical decision of philosophy, that anything is philosophizable. See, for instance, the opening sections of his *Principles of Non-philosophy*, trans. Anthony Paul Smith and Nicola Rubczak (New York: Bloomsbury, 2013).

109. James Heisig's book *Philosophers of Nothingness: An Essay on the Kyoto School* (Honolulu: University of Hawaii Press, 2002) is one of the most cogent appraisals of this under-read philosophical tradition. My analysis draws extensively from his book. For a sampling of Kyoto School writings, see the anthology *The Buddha Eye: An Anthology of the Kyoto School*, ed. Frederick Franck (World View Press, 2004). For a broader view of Japanese philosophy, see *Japanese Philosophy: A Sourcebook*, ed. James Heisig et al. (Honolulu: University of Hawaii Press, 2011) and Heinrich Dumolin, *Zen Buddhism in the 20th Century*, trans. Joseph O'Leary (New York: Weatherhill, 1992).

110. Masao Abe, *Zen and Western Thought*, ed. William R. LaFleur (Honolulu: University of Hawaii Press, 1989), p. 133.

111. For the sake of consistency I will be referring to Japanese authors with the family name last and given name first.

112. Nagarjuna, *The Fundamental Wisdom of the Middle Way*, trans. Jay Garfield (Oxford: Oxford University Press, 1995), XXII.11, p. 61.

113. Ibid., XIII.7, p. 36.

114. Quoted in Heisig, *Philosophers of Nothingness*, p. 44.

115. Ibid., p. 48.

116. Ibid., p. 63.

117. One of the issues that Heisig discusses throughout his book is the often confused and conflicted relation between philosophy and politics in modern Japan, particularly

surrounding the Kyoto School's flirtations with nationalism. Heisig neither excuses nor condemns the Kyoto School's attempts to link philosophy with politics, and, interestingly, religion often comes to serve as a mediator between them.

118. Nishitani, *The Self-Overcoming of Nihilism*, trans. Graham Parkes with Setsuko Aihara (Albany: SUNY, 1990), p. 175.

119. Keiji Nishitani, *Religion and Nothingness*, trans. Jan Van Bragt (Berkeley: University of California Press, 1983), p. 4.

120. Ibid., p. 48.

121. Ibid., pp. 17-18.

122. Ibid., p. 112.

123. Ibid., p. 90.

124. Ibid.

125. Ibid., p. 96.

126. Ibid., p. 137.

127. Ibid., p. 138.

128. Ibid., p. 97.

129. Ibid., pp. 96-97.

130. Ibid., p. 123.

131. Heisig, pp. 220-21.

132. Ibid., p. 221.

133. Abe, *Zen and Western Thought*, pp. 126-27.

134. Shizuteru Ueda, "'Nothingness' in Meister Eckhart and Zen Buddhism," trans. James Heisig, in *The Buddha Eye: An Anthology of the Kyoto School*, ed. Frederick Franck (New York: Crossroad, 1982), pp. 160, 161.

135. Ibid., p. 230.

136. Ibid., p. 61.

137. The widespread coverage of extremophile research is evidenced by pop science books like Michael Ray Taylor's *Dark Life: Martian Nanobacteria, Rock-Eating Cave Bugs, and Other Extreme Organisms of Inner Earth and Outer Space* (New York: Scribner, 1999), as well as a number of science documentaries, including *Journey into Amazing Caves*. There

is a college-level textbook *Physiology and Biochemistry of Extremophiles* (Washington D.C.: ASM Press, 2007), and there even exists a number of professional organizations, such as the International Society for Extremophiles.

138. European Science Foundation (ESF), *Investigating Life in Extreme Environments – A European Perspective* (Strasbourg: European Science Foundation, 2007), p. 13. See also the press release from NASA (December 2010), announcing the discovery of an arsenic-based bacterium: http://www.nasa.gov/home/hqnews/2010/dec/HQ_10-320_Toxic_Life.html.

139. Ibid., p. 15.

140. "Gold Mine Holds Life Untouched by Sun," *New Scientist* (19 October 2006).

141. Benjamin Noys, *The Persistence of the Negative* (Edinburgh: Edinburgh University Press, 2010), p. ix. Extending Noys' comments, we might add that cultural theory follows suit in its affirmationism of the particularities and contingencies of social, economic, and political identities, just as science studies follows suit with its affirmationism of "chaotic" and "complex" generative systems in the natural world.

142. Ibid.

143. For an accessible overview, see Graham Priest, *Beyond the Limits of Thought* (Oxford: Oxford University Press, 2003).

144. Laruelle, *Principles of Non-philosophy*, p. 2, italics removed.

145. Ludwig Wittgenstein, *Tractatus Logico-Philosophicus*, ed. and trans. D.F. Pears and B.F. McGuinness (New York: Routledge & Keegan Paul, 1961), 4.0621, p. 45.

146. Ibid.

147. Kant never says so, but one is tempted to state it: Life is noumenal.

148. I will be using the phrases "post-Kantian Idealism" and "German Idealism" interchangeably, though arguably there are reasons for treating them as separate terms.

149. The most frequently-referenced example is in the opening sections of the *Phenomenology of Spirit,* though the *Philosophy of Nature,* part of Hegel's *Encyclopedia of the Philosophical Sciences,* also revisits these themes, from the perspective of Nature as manifest Spirit.

150. Schelling returned again and again to this relationship between Nature and the Absolute, from earlier works such as the *First Outline of a System of the Philosophy of Nature,* to his later work *The Ages of the World.*

151. This phrase plays a key role in Fichte's lectures, some of which are collected in *The Science of Knowing – Fichte's 1804 Lectures on the Wissenshaftslehre.*

152. Here I borrow Steven Shaviro's paraphrase of Whitehead's process philosophy in his book *Without Criteria* (Cambridge: MIT Press, 2012), though used here in a different context.

153. On life-as-genesis, see Bergson's *Creative Evolution,* as well as nearly all of Deleuze's work, including *Bergsonism, Difference and Repetition,* and the two volumes of *Cinema.* On life-as-givenness, see Jean-Luc Marion's *Being Given: Towards a Phenomenology of Givenness,* and Michel Henry's multi-volume *Phenomenology of Life.*

154. There is an anecdote often told about Schopenhauer that, while lecturing in Berlin in 1820, intentionally chose the same time for his lectures as that of Hegel. Needless to say, the latter continued to draw huge crowds, while the former was faced with an empty hall.

155. *The World as Will and Representation,* Volume I, trans. E.F.J. Payne (New York: Dover, 1969), p. 429.

156. Ibid., 434, italics removed.

157. Ibid., pp. 25-26.

158. Ibid., p. 3.

159. Ibid., p. 124.

160. Ibid., p. 19.

161. Ibid., p. 4.

162. Ibid., p. 417, italics removed.

163. Ibid., Vol. II, p. 579.

164. Ibid., Vol. I, p. 275. I have chosen to translate Schopenhauer's *Wille zum Leben* as Will-to-Life. However the Payne translation renders it "will-to-live."

165. This is one of the greatest lessons of Cartesianism prior to Schopenhauer, and of phenomenology after Schopenhauer.

166. *The World as Will and Representation*, Vol. I, §18, p. 100.

167. Ibid.

168. Ibid., pp. 102-103.

169. Ibid., p. 275.

170. Schopenhauer's negative approach is a position that is as much about being a curmudgeon as it is about critique – indeed the stylistic innovation in Schopenhauer's writings is to have rendered the two inseparable, culminating in a form of philosophical pessimism.

171. *The World as Will and Representation*, Vol. I., p. 146-47.

172. Ibid., p. 147.

173. Ibid., p. 149.

174. Ibid., p. 113.

175. Ibid., pp. 159-60.

176. Ibid., p. 322.

177. Ibid., p. 162.

178. On Schopenhauer's complicated relation to Eastern philosophy, see Peter Abelsen, "Schopenhauer and Buddhism," *Philosophy East and West* 43:2 (1993): 255-78; and Moira Nicholls, "The Influences of Eastern Thought on Schopenhauer's Doctrine of the Thing-in-Itself," in *The Cambridge Companion to Schopenhauer*, ed. Christopher Janaway (Cambridge: Cambridge University Press, 1999), pp. 171-212.

179. *The World as Will and Representation*, Vol. I, p. 410.

180. Ibid., p. 409.

181. Ibid., p. 412.

182. We could also take some lessons from the not-so-high culture of cartoons. Take the case of Glum, one of the characters in *The Adventures of Gulliver*, a cartoon produced by Hanna-Barbera in the 1970s. In the cartoon, Glum was notorious for his pessimistic outlook, expressed in his monotone, droll phraseology: "We'll never make it..." or simply "We're doomed..." Glum not only stood out from his more optimistic, idealistic and chivalric counterparts (which was basically everyone else in Gulliver's crew), but he often had the knack of delivering his pessimistic proclamations just when they would be the most unhelpful (when taken prisoner, when drowning at sea, even when free-falling from a cliff); that is, when the gloomy fate of the adventurers seemed to be *obvious* beyond stating. Never mind that Gulliver's crew seemed to be miraculously saved at the end of each episode; even the miracle itself was not enough to convert Glum, who never ceased to remark on the futility of all action. Glum is the dark stain on the glossy veneer of an ethics reduced to self-help. And yet he, like Candide, continues to go along with things.

183. The Cambridge Edition of the works of Schopenhauer, edited by Christopher Janaway, is making available modern, scholarly translations of Schopenhauer's works. For years, those reading Schopenhauer in English have had to make do with the Dover editions which, while important, left something to be desired for the student and scholar. In addition, the advent of inexpensive, print-on-demand technologies has issued in a flurry of Schopenhauer reprints, but with varying degrees of editorial quality – many are marred by poor copyediting, uneven translation and even poor page layout and design. Given this, this series is a welcome intervention.

184. Schopenhauer, *The Two Fundamental Problems of Ethics*, ed. and trans. Christopher Janaway (Cambridge: Cambridge

University Press, 2009), p. 36.

185. Ibid., p. 63.

186. Ibid., p. 125.

187. Ibid., p. 129.

188. Ibid., p. 148. Given this critique, Schopenhauer does rescue certain elements of Kant's ethical philosophy. In particular, Schopenhauer does something interesting with the freedom-necessity pair he had already examined in the first essay. Necessity, as sufficient ground, is an extension of the phenomenal world of appearance, the domain of the individuated human will, what Schopenhauer calls the "empirical character" of the human being. To this is contrasted freedom, which Schopenhauer had already defined in terms of absolute contingency, and which he allies with the Kantian noumenal world, the Will in itself that is nevertheless manifest in the human being, what Schopenhauer calls the "intelligible character."

189. Ibid., p. 174.

190. There are a number of historical overviews of philosophical pessimism, many of which were written in the 19th century aftermath of Schopenhauer's popularity, and which are still of interest for contemporary readers. These include James Sully's *Pessimism: A History and a Criticism* (1877), Elme-Marie Caro's *Le pessimisme au XIXème siècle* (1878), Edouard von Hartmann's *Zur Geschichte und Begründung des Pessimismus* (1880), Edgar Saltus' *The Philosophy of Disenchantment* (1885), and Robert Mark Wenley's *Aspects of Pessimism* (1894), to name a few. A recent study is Joshua Foa Deinstag's 2009 book *Pessimism: Philosophy, Ethic, Spirit*.

191. Cosmic pessimism is further explored in my text "Cosmic Pessimism," published in *continent* 2.2 (2012), and in the first volume of this series, *In the Dust of This Planet*, pp. 16ff.

192. Steven Shaviro, "Panpsychism and/or Eliminativism," paper delivered at the Third Object Oriented Ontology conference,

9 September 2011, The New School, New York. A video of the lecture is available at: http://www.ustream.tv/rec orded/17269234. It appears that some of the material from the lecture is taken from Shaviro's work-in-progress, an experimental science fiction novel entitled *Noosphere*.

193. Shaviro specifically cites Negarestani's *Cyclonopedia*, my books *After Life* and *In the Dust Of This Planet*, and Woodard's "dark vitalism" project – to which we might also add Ray Brassier's *Nihil Unbound* and Thomas Ligotti's *The Conspiracy Against the Human Race*.

194. For an innovative critique and extension of eliminativism, see the first chapter of Ray Brassier's *Nihil Unbound: Enlightenment and Extinction* (London: Palgrave, 2007).

195. As contemporary philosophy seems to be particular fond of branding, one could coin new terms for this type of eliminativism: "dark eliminativism," "black eliminativism," "eliminative eliminativism," "the Ab-human Eliminativism of the Watching Mists" and so on.

196. This is not meant as a dismissal, simply a provocation. Consider the following as case studies: the role of Fichte in Quentin Meillassoux's *After Finitude*, the role of Schelling in Iain Hamilton Grant's *Philosophies of Nature After Schelling* and the edited volume *The New Schelling* (ed. Judith Norman and Alistair Welchman); and the role of that greatest of resurrected corpses, Hegel, in works such as Jean-Luc Nancy's *Hegel: The Restlessness of the Negative*, and Catherine Malabou's *The Future of Hegel: Plasticity, Time, and the Dialectic*.

197. Novalis, *Pollen and Fragments*, trans. Arthur Versluis (Grand Rapids: Phanes, 1989), p. 70.

198. Figures from the World Health Organization (WHO).

199. Figures from Stuart Pimm, *A Scientist Audits the Earth* (New Brunswick: Rutgers University Press, 2004).

200. Ray Brassier, *Nihil Unbound: Enlightenment and Extinction*, p.

223, italics removed.

201. Ibid.

202. Ibid.

203. Ibid., pp. 229-30.

204. This is what Brassier, borrowing from Sellars, calls the "manifest" and "scientific" images of the world.

205. Brassier, *Nihil Unbound*, p. 229.

206. Ibid., p. xi.

207. Ibid.

208. Ibid.

209. Friedrich Nietzsche, *Human, All Too Human (I)*, pp. 15-16.

210. Pascal, *Pensées*, trans. A.J. Krailsheimer (New York: Penguin, 1966), Fragment #199, p. 88.

211. Ibid., p. 89.

212. Ibid., pp. 89-90.

213. Ibid., p. 89

214. Ibid.

215. Ibid.

216. Brassier, *Nihil Unbound*, p. 228.

Contemporary culture has eliminated both the concept of the public and the figure of the intellectual. Former public spaces – both physical and cultural – are now either derelict or colonized by advertising. A cretinous anti-intellectualism presides, cheerled by expensively educated hacks in the pay of multinational corporations who reassure their bored readers that there is no need to rouse themselves from their interpassive stupor. The informal censorship internalized and propagated by the cultural workers of late capitalism generates a banal conformity that the propaganda chiefs of Stalinism could only ever have dreamt of imposing. Zer0 Books knows that another kind of discourse – intellectual without being academic, popular without being populist – is not only possible: it is already flourishing, in the regions beyond the striplit malls of so-called mass media and the neurotically bureaucratic halls of the academy. Zer0 is committed to the idea of publishing as a making public of the intellectual. It is convinced that in the unthinking, blandly consensual culture in which we live, critical and engaged theoretical reflection is more important than ever before.

ZERO BOOKS

If this book has helped you to clarify an idea, solve a problem or extend your knowledge, you may like to read more titles from Zero Books. Recent bestsellers are:

Capitalist Realism Is there no alternative?
Mark Fisher
An analysis of the ways in which capitalism has presented itself as the only realistic political-economic system.
Paperback: November 27, 2009 978-1-84694-317-1 $14.95 £7.99.
eBook: July 1, 2012 978-1-78099-734-6 $9.99 £6.99.

The Wandering Who? A study of Jewish identity politics
Gilad Atzmon
An explosive unique crucial book tackling the issues of Jewish Identity Politics and ideology and their global influence.
Paperback: September 30, 2011 978-1-84694-875-6 $14.95 £8.99.
eBook: September 30, 2011 978-1-84694-876-3 $9.99 £6.99.

Clampdown Pop-cultural wars on class and gender
Rhian E. Jones
Class and gender in Britpop and after, and why 'chav' is a feminist issue.
Paperback: March 29, 2013 978-1-78099-708-7 $14.95 £9.99.
eBook: March 29, 2013 978-1-78099-707-0 $7.99 £4.99.

The Quadruple Object
Graham Harman
Uses a pack of playing cards to present Harman's metaphysical system of fourfold objects, including human access, Heidegger's indirect causation, panpsychism and ontography.
Paperback: July 29, 2011 978-1-84694-700-1 $16.95 £9.99.

Weird Realism Lovecraft and Philosophy
Graham Harman
As Hölderlin was to Martin Heidegger and Mallarmé to Jacques
Derrida, so is H.P. Lovecraft to the Speculative Realist philoso-
phers.
Paperback: September 28, 2012 978-1-78099-252-5 $24.95 £14.99.
eBook: September 28, 2012 978-1-78099-907-4 $9.99 £6.99.

Sweetening the Pill or How We Got Hooked on Hormonal Birth
Control
Holly Grigg-Spall
Is it really true? Has contraception liberated or oppressed
women?
Paperback: September 27, 2013 978-1-78099-607-3 $22.95 £12.99.
eBook: September 27, 2013 978-1-78099-608-0 $9.99 £6.99.

Why Are We The Good Guys? Reclaiming Your Mind From The
Delusions Of Propaganda
David Cromwell
A provocative challenge to the standard ideology that Western
power is a benevolent force in the world.
Paperback: September 28, 2012 978-1-78099-365-2 $26.95 £15.99.
eBook: September 28, 2012 978-1-78099-366-9 $9.99 £6.99.

The Truth about Art Reclaiming quality
Patrick Doorly
The book traces the multiple meanings of art to their various
sources, and equips the reader to choose between them.
Paperback: August 30, 2013 978-1-78099-841-1 $32.95 £19.99.

Bells and Whistles More Speculative Realism
Graham Harman
In this diverse collection of sixteen essays, lectures, and inter-
views Graham Harman lucidly explains the principles of

Speculative Realism, including his own object-oriented philosophy.
Paperback: November 29, 2013 978-1-78279-038-9 $26.95 £15.99.
eBook: November 29, 2013 978-1-78279-037-2 $9.99 £6.99.

Towards Speculative Realism: Essays and Lectures Essays and Lectures
Graham Harman
These writings chart Harman's rise from Chicago sportswriter to co founder of one of Europe's most promising philosophical movements: Speculative Realism.
Paperback: November 26, 2010 978-1-84694-394-2 $16.95 £9.99.
eBook: January 1, 1970 978-1-84694-603-5 $9.99 £6.99.

Meat Market Female flesh under capitalism
Laurie Penny
A feminist dissection of women's bodies as the fleshy fulcrum of capitalist cannibalism, whereby women are both consumers and consumed.
Paperback: April 29, 2011 978-1-84694-521-2 $12.95 £6.99.
eBook: May 21, 2012 978-1-84694-782-7 $9.99 £6.99.

Translating Anarchy The Anarchism of Occupy Wall Street
Mark Bray
An insider's account of the anarchists who ignited Occupy Wall Street.
Paperback: September 27, 2013 978-1-78279-126-3 $26.95 £15.99.
eBook: September 27, 2013 978-1-78279-125-6 $6.99 £4.99.

One Dimensional Woman
Nina Power
Exposes the dark heart of contemporary cultural life by examining pornography, consumer capitalism and the ideology of women's work.

Paperback: November 27, 2009 978-1-84694-241-9 $14.95 £7.99.
eBook: July 1, 2012 978-1-78099-737-7 $9.99 £6.99.

Dead Man Working
Carl Cederstrom, Peter Fleming
An analysis of the dead man working and the way in which
capital is now colonizing life itself.
Paperback: May 25, 2012 978-1-78099-156-6 $14.95 £9.99.
eBook: June 27, 2012 978-1-78099-157-3 $9.99 £6.99.

Unpatriotic History of the Second World War
James Heartfield
The Second World War was not the Good War of legend. James
Heartfield explains that both Allies and Axis powers fought for
the same goals - territory, markets and natural resources.
Paperback: September 28, 2012 978-1-78099-378-2 $42.95 £23.99.
eBook: September 28, 2012 978-1-78099-379-9 $9.99 £6.99.

Find more titles at www.zero-books.net